Also by Susan Altschwager

An Ordinary Woman's Extraordinary Journey (2001)

NEW STORY

FOR HUMANITY

Susan Altschwager

BALBOA.
PRESS

A DIVISION OF HAY HOUSE

Balboa Press books may be ordered through booksellers or by contacting:

Balboa Press
A Division of Hay House
1663 Liberty Drive
Bloomington, IN 47403
www.balboapress.com.au
1-(877) 407-4847

ISBN: 978-1-4525-1116-0 (sc)
ISBN: 978-1-4525-1117-7 (e)

Because of the dynamic nature of the Internet, any web addresses or links contained in this book may have changed since publication and may no longer be valid. The views expressed in this work are solely those of the author and do not necessarily reflect the views of the publisher, and the publisher hereby disclaims any responsibility for them.

The author of this book does not dispense medical advice or prescribe the use of any technique as a form of treatment for physical, emotional, or medical problems without the advice of a physician, either directly or indirectly. The intent of the author is only to offer information of a general nature to help you in your quest for emotional and spiritual well-being. In the event you use any of the information in this book for yourself, which is your constitutional right, the author and the publisher assume no responsibility for your actions.

Any people depicted in stock imagery provided by Thinkstock are models, and such images are being used for illustrative purposes only.
Certain stock imagery © Thinkstock.

Printed in the United States of America

Balboa Press rev. date: 08/05/2013

To the new pioneers of today. They have been working so hard over the last few decades as ordinary people, committed women and men who have heard a deep call inside them. As a small percentage of the population globally, you have walked a journey of transformation and change. There were no instructions for you to follow, your intuition being your guiding light and a knowing that you trusted. Many times your own truth was in opposition to the truth of the day, and it has taken courage and strength for you to walk your journey. You have been in service for humanity, opened a doorway, as behind that doorway was a race of people in prison—the human race. In 2012, the doorway fully opened, and new leaders are being asked to stand up and take humanity's hand while walking through the doorway to a new story, a birth of a new humanity.

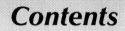

Contents

Acknowledgments

I wrote this book because I had encouragement and much support from fellow practitioners to own and stand in my truth with this information, as they believe it is important to share it with more people. It was suggested to either take my book, *An Ordinary Woman's Extraordinary Journey*, and stand with it or expand some of the information into a new book. I have grown a lot since my first book, and I felt I could participate more fully without any fear. I was thinking of the amount of work that would be needed to rewrite my book, as I don't see myself as a writer because I'm dyslexic. In the same week that I was considering writing a new book, I went to lunch with a friend, Cindy, and I expressed what was happening to me and this idea of writing and expanding on my first book. Cindy went silent and eventually with tears in her eyes said, "It would be my honour to help you with the writing." I thought, *Oh my God, I'm going to have to do it now*. It was like we were being guided, looked after, and it was destiny.

I acknowledge the many people that have been a part of my life journey, giving me support, inspiration, and love. My friends that were there at the beginning of my activation, new people that came into my life, supporting me to walk forward, all the women that stood beside me when I wrote my first book. A special thanks to Cindy Pellas for her commitment and love in providing me with skills that enabled me to create *New Story for Humanity*. And to Lucy Deslandes's artistic attribute in designing the book cover.

My parents, Norm and Mary Mitchell, who have both passed away, because of you I stand with this love and light to share with many. I love you both.

My beautiful family, husband, children and their partners, grandchildren, I love you all. You are the most important people in my life.

To the place I was born, family and friends I will always hold close in my heart.

Love and gratitude to all the pioneers who have come into my life.

Introduction

I am an ordinary woman, a daughter, a sister, a wife, a mother, a grandmother, and a friend. Twenty-five years ago, I was living my life like many of you who live in the Western world. I was living in a small country town in southeast South Australia, and I was busy creating a life around my family, my home, my career, and my community. I was not searching for the answers to life, and I was very happy with the life I lived.

Then I experienced phenomena that changed my life forever. I was out in nature one day and had an interaction with a non-physical being called Anton. It happened in a matter of seconds. He was a gatekeeper for an ancient temple. This interaction caused me to have profound changes in my reality, as at the time of this experience, my reality was family, fashion, and friends. There was an acceleration of heightened frequency within me. I opened and travelled through a doorway, experiencing a very powerful vortex of electromagnetic energy. I participated in a journey that took me to places I did not know existed.

Ancient wisdom and knowledge lie underneath the Earth's bed under a time release of evolution. Ancient temples, electromagnetic energy fields, and evolution were not a part of my vocabulary. It has taken many years to find the words to explain the experience. What I understood at the beginning was that I was hit with a force field. It was very physical, and I instantly opened up to knowledge that I had no idea about. I didn't know how I knew this information, and I was not hearing a voice. It was this deep knowing in me, and it was louder than any thought I could think. At the beginning, I would tell myself, "If you believe any of this knowing, you will go mad." I was overwhelmed.

I have been on an amazing journey of change, transformation, acceptance, surrender, and now peace over the last twenty-five years. The information that birthed in me did not come from a source outside of me, as my DNA codes were activated when the electromagnetic force field aligned in me. This gave me insight into my evolution and the human cycle of life on Mother Earth. The knowing was so strong that it was not a thought; it was deeper, and in fact, my thoughts did not want any of this. I was happy in the world that I knew and understood. I was in a great deal of fear, as I had no idea what was happening to me. I yelled, I screamed, I swore, and I cried. I went to a place inside me where I felt I could not breathe in the same breath as the present human reality of existence. I felt like I left the present world, and I did not want what was happening to me.

This is very difficult to understand coming from the intellect of human logic. I felt totally alienated from the people and places that I loved, yet Mother Earth's secrets opened to me. I held on so tightly to keep my sanity, and it was the love of my family that kept me grounded. I could feel the pain inside from my own separation and the pain of humanity. I felt I was forced to let go and surrender. There was no choice, and I had no control over what was happening to me. I could feel the disconnection from my being, and I could see that what I loved and believed to be my truth was my separation.

We are at a time in our evolution where a bigger picture is being exposed to us, and this process is natural and our birth right. We will begin to understand that the power source within us is our heart. The electromagnetic force field is more powerful than any thought form. The heart is the place of connection to each other, to Mother Earth, and galactic worlds. Humanity is at a time of completion and at the end of how we understand our human existence. We are also at a time of birth of a new story and a new way of living on Mother Earth.

Humanity is at a time of great change, and we have reached a crossroad where we have global issues, climate change, population growth, devaluation of human life, and depletion of resources that are affecting the whole human race. Many of the structures that have provided us with answers and stability are in a process of change. There needs to be education about the changes so that people can live through this time of change and transition without fear, by having information about a new story being birthed for the human race. We are not at a time of destruction although many of our old structures are at a time of completion. We are at a time of expansion. Something big is happening on Mother Earth.

The old story, the way we have existed and lived life in this present world, and the history of humanity has been in a place of separation and disconnection. The intellect, the thought process, has continually expanded throughout history, creating the life we live today. We are more than a thought, so it is not our thoughts that have the answers. We are being asked to evolve to new heights of reality, yet it is the thought, the intellect, that has control over who we think we are. We have reached a time when we have the ability to understand a bigger picture of human reality. The crisis that we are facing as a human race has the opportunity to take us to this bigger picture. We will need to expand our thinking and open our hearts to provide the world we live in with new solutions for our global issues.

There are many ordinary men and women globally who have their own stories of expansion and transformation and are seeing life in a new way. Pioneers of our time have heard the winds of change deep inside of them to make a difference. They have been working extremely hard over the last few decades and are a small percentage of the global population feeling the pulsating evolution, calling to them to open a doorway for humanity to walk through.

Ordinary Woman's Extraordinary Journey

*I allowed myself connection
to Mother Earth.
We were invisible to one another.
A higher order of consciousness has
linked us together, freeing me from
the bonds of human reality.
I am able to see and know all that is.
This location is in my heart.
Alignment of my will with purest love:
this is a commitment to the
highest truth of my being.*

1

An Ordinary Woman's Extraordinary Journey

Change is a part of all of our lives; it is experienced in many different ways and often brings with it growth and looking at life in a different way. I was born in a small country town in the southeast of South Australia, where I lived with both of my parents, my brother, and my two sisters. I was the eldest sibling in my family. My father was a rational and logical man, and my mother had a great love that she shared freely with all of us. I feel I have taken on these qualities, and I thank my parents for passing them onto me. Growing up in this small, country community, I felt safe and protected. My primary school years were spent at a Catholic convent, and religion was my favourite subject. My secondary years were at the public school in the small country town.

At sixteen, I left school to be employed in a fashion store. I had met my husband, Wally, whom I married when I was nineteen years old, and we have now been married for over forty years. We built our home in the country town and settled into a life that I believed would always remain. I loved living in this country town. Our first child was stillborn, and I remember this time as extremely painful for both of us. Over the next ten years, we were blessed with three beautiful, healthy babies, one daughter and two sons. My husband and I were firmly committed to building our dreams in this small community. Our home was always full of family and friends. My life looked and felt good, and I had my own business in the fashion retail industry for over twelve years.

I was not looking for the answers to life. I was not searching for a deeper meaning to human existence. I introduce myself as an ordinary woman, and this is not to deplete who I am; it is to tell you who I am. I lived like many millions of other women in Australia, with similar beliefs, conditions, dreams, and desires for themselves and their families.

When I was pregnant with my youngest son, I became friends with another woman who was pregnant at the same time. Her son and mine became buddies growing up together. She was very open-minded and different from my other friends. She practiced meditation and other modalities that were not part of my reality. For example, she had been visiting a particular site in the Adelaide Hills to mediate, and she told me that there was an ancient site there. I didn't believe her, and I thought she was different!

In May 1989, I went to Adelaide with her and another woman for a weekend. I went to do some buying for my business while the two other women participated in a mediation workshop. I had finished my buying on the Saturday, and the women invited me to attend the workshop the next day. Even though I had no understanding of what mediation was about, the adventurous part of me was curious, so I went.

At the workshop, the facilitator told us to close our eyes, as we were going to the centre of the Earth. I didn't believe a word he said, but I did what I was told, being the good girl that I was. As I closed my eyes and followed all the instructions he was saying, which included going to a pre-civilisation and to the centre of the Earth, I remember going to a place where I met a man. I felt frightened, as I had never meditated before, and a part of me didn't believe what I was doing. The thought of a civilisation in the centre of the Earth was ridiculous to me. I did not see a civilisation in my meditation, yet I know I connected to someone. I felt it; there was no communication. I did not understand it, and I felt out of my comfort zone, so I quickly opened my eyes and came out of the meditation.

The next day on our way home, I had a feeling inside me, and the words just came out before I even had time to connect to them. I asked if the ancient site where they meditated in the Adelaide Hills was very far away. With that, my friend turned the car around and said, "It's not far," and before I knew it, we were there. We arrived at Horsnell Gully, which the Aborigines call the Serpentine Trail. The symbol for the Serpentine is the snake, and it means transformation.

Then something happened to change my life forever. I call it a phenomenon because it had absolutely no logical explanation. As destiny unfolded for me, I found myself walking the Serpentine Trail with the two friends I had come to Adelaide with. They were taking me to the ancient temple that they had meditated on in previous weeks. My attitude at the time was, *What the hell am I doing here?* We walked about a kilometre, and my friend said, "We're here," indicating that we were at the ancient site. I wondered how she knew that because the environment didn't look any different from the rest of the area that we had walked. My friend started climbing up on some rocks that were quite high, and I decided to just sit because I was tired and had enough already.

Sitting by myself in that very quiet place in nature, I felt very still. I was not in a meditative state; I just felt very still, an unusual experience for me. Then a figure of a man, not of present-day appearance, presented himself to me. His voice said, "My name is Anton. I am not your teacher. I am here to give you transformation for humanity." I couldn't physically touch him if I reached out, and he seemed to be about five metres away from me. He appeared to be a projection, and I wasn't sure if he was real or not. He had golden skin and strawberry-blond, shoulder-length hair, and he was clothed in a white toga, a thin golden band around his head, thick golden bands around his wrists, and sandals on his feet. He was a beautiful, handsome man who seemed to be ageless, and he emitted a golden energy. He appeared to be in front of a river, and this interaction was quick, lasting only seconds.

I was not sure if this experience was internal or external. I felt that it was external, and I found that hard to believe. Before the two women came back to me, I picked up three rocks from this place and put them in my pocket. Neither of the two women said anything to me, and I did not share what I experienced with them because I didn't think I really believed it myself. I came home and told my husband what had happened and what I had experienced. He said, "Different people experience different things." I did not take the visitation as something important; I did not know how real it was. It was when the next part of my journey started to unfold that I started to acknowledge the visitation as real.

I've never had communication or interaction with this being Anton again. Through my own growth and the expansion of my reality, I began to accept and understand that Anton was a gatekeeper from an ancient civilisation. These beings of light from this ancient civilisation are here to help the transformation of humanity. I did not have this information or awareness at the time of my experience with Anton. There is so much we as a race of people do not understand about ourselves or this amazing planet, Mother Earth.

I got on with my life, not mentioning the visitation to anyone else. Within a few weeks, I was on another buying trip for my fashion business, and two women who worked for me, Kay and Jane, came to help choose fashion clothing for the next season. That night, we stayed in a motel in the city, and when I turned off the lights, one of the girls, Kay, screamed and said she saw a white light all over me. She said, "Susan, you're here to give humanity something," and then she said, "I don't even know why I said that. It just came out." Even though I could see both girls were very frightened, I didn't know if I believed that they saw anything. They jumped into bed with me and said, "Please don't go to sleep." They were too scared to close their eyes. We did not sleep that night, and when one of us needed to go to the toilet, we all went. That's how frightened they were.

At this time, both the girls' reality included reading romantic novels, their family, and having good social times. We all liked the same lifestyle. The next day, we were all confused and tired, but we continued_buying clothing for the next season. I trusted the girls'

4

buying experience, so I told them to go to a different section from where I was buying to do some buying for next season's fashions. Within half an hour, they came back, and Kay was as white as a ghost. She said, "What's happening to me?" And then she said, "Ask me a question." She said that every time someone asked her if she wanted a particular item of clothing, her body would sway left to right for a no and forward and back for a yes answer. I didn't understand what she was saying, and I even felt perhaps she was exaggerating. During the rest of the day, she didn't appear to be her normal self. She was agitated and talking about how she felt our lives were changing and that I would be doing something different than working with fashion. She was raving, and she had never talked like that before. I was questioning what was going on, and I wondered if it was all real.

On the way home, as we got closer, Kay slid off the front passenger seat under the dash in a foetal position and started sobbing and saying that she couldn't go home to her husband like this. Then she said "Sue, get it out of me. It's to do with you." When I saw the fear in her, I stopped thinking what was going on was not real.

I had no idea what to do, so I yelled, "If this is anything to do with me, get out of her." Instantly it left her, and even though she was exhausted, she felt she was able to go home. She seemed calmer, had stopped the raving, and was back to herself. When I took Kay home, she said she was feeling okay and was able to face her husband.

Two days later, Sue, a lifelong friend who also worked for me, was in my kitchen with me when Kay phoned to say she was coming to visit. When Kay arrived, she said, "I don't feel the energy is in me anymore, but there is something peculiar still happening to me. I don't even feel like I drove the car here." I didn't understand what she was saying, as the logical part of me couldn't accept this and I could see she was upset.

All three of us sat around my kitchen table feeling a little scared and vulnerable. It felt unreal, and then Kay banged on the table and said, "I am demanding answers!" She was really forceful, and with that, I instantly felt a very powerful energy force penetrate my body.

It was like megawatts of electricity, and my whole body was filled with this electricity. It was difficult for me to move physically at first, as I felt heavy and slow. I started saying to the girls, "My God, we are going to go through massive changes on Earth." I just started to speak about information having to do with activation and transformation on the planet. I had no idea how I knew what I was saying. I just had to express myself, as I could not hold it back. The energy erupted within me like a volcano, and it activated and transferred to the girls. As a result of Anton's visitation, I became a vortex for this vibration, and the girls received an activation from me. The three of us were overwhelmed and felt a great deal of disbelief about what was happening. I spoke to my husband when he came home that night and showed him the energy in my body. Both of us had no explanation or realisation of the journey that was head of us.

From that day sitting around my kitchen table, Sue received the vibration in a gentle and powerful process. As she was activated, her whole body was moving and swaying. She seemed scared, and like me, she didn't believe what was happening. She has been on an amazing journey of change and transformation over the last twenty-five years. She is a pioneer of our times to have accepted and held this vibration frequency for the purpose of transformation for humanity. Initially, she didn't fully understand what was happening and often questioned the reality of what she was experiencing and whether it was real or not. However, as a result of this experience, her eyesight changed, and now Sue can look at a person's body and see what is out of balance.

I believe this is a gift. Some would call her a medical intuitive. About two years ago when we were both in Queensland, I was in awe of the gift she has. Sue is able to heal with her eyes. When she is healing someone, I have witnessed a blue energy field going up a person's arm as Sue's eyes move up with the energy, without her physically touching the body. We have remained great friends, and Sue has always supported me in my journey.

The same thing happened to Kay. The vibration in her body was gentle, and like Sue, it introduced her to a whole new world. Looking back, I can see Kay was originally activated back in the hotel room where she saw the white light around me. As a result of both experiences, Kay became extremely frightened, lost huge amounts of weight, and had a breakdown. I would now call this a spiritual crisis. Over time, she became stable, and although she has endured the experience on her own without exposing her journey to anyone around her, this vibration has never left her. She is a pioneer of our time, enduring and holding a vibrational frequency that she has no true understanding about and living as normal a life as possible with her family and friends in silence.

As for Jane, she was the youngest of all the women that worked for me. She had a great awareness and held the space in the fashion shop whilst I and the other women went through the beginnings of our journey. She now lives in NSW, is married with a beautiful daughter, and has great acceptance and understanding of what we all went through.

At the time, we had no conscious understanding as to what was happening to us. I could doubt the experience with Anton, as it could just have been in my head, but I could not doubt the physical changes that were happening to me and the girls. My hands and body would often shake and rock, and it could be physically seen by others. It was a physical, mental, and emotion experience for Kay, Sue, and me. This vibrational energy touched all the girls who worked for me, including my two sisters. The activation touched this small group of women and no one else.

Anne was a friend from high school, and she also worked in my Mt. Gambier fashion shop with another woman called Judy. Their process of activation was much slower and happened through daily interactions and communication about what had happened to me and the other girls. They were slowly pulled into the activation and introduced to the different knowledge. For example, Judy became interested in UFOs and extra-terrestrials. She had not been interested in any of this before.

One day, Judy came to see me because she was worried about Anne, as she was acting strangely, so I drove to visit Anne. When I saw her,

I immediately felt she was not her usual self. She was normally a light and gentle person. She was stern faced, serious, and I noticed she wasn't wearing any makeup. She had a scarf over her head, and her whole presence was different. She felt distant, and I said, "Anne, this energy isn't what this is all about." Instantly she snapped out of what she was feeling, removed the scarf, yelled to her family not to listen to her about any of this, and her gentle presence returned.

We then sat down together, and she told me what had been happening to her for the last twenty-four to forty-eight hours. Her experience was so powerful and overwhelming that she felt the energy force had taken over her and her family. She demanded that her family pray in the early hours of the morning and night and at specific times of the day. They were not to eat meat, were to wear crosses around their neck, and everything needed to be scrubbed and cleaned. She was doing things she had never done in her life, like wanting to wear a scarf over her head. It felt like she was becoming a Muslim, which was strange, seeing as she was a Christian. What amazed and scared her was that her family listened to her and did what she suggested. This experience lasted for a short time but stayed in her memory for a long time. It still scares her to this day, and I don't understand it fully.

I believe she could have gone back into a past life. She spent a lot of her energy trying to stop what was happening. When this energy first activated within her, it was very powerful, and she said it felt like something was controlling her. Since then, she has done a lot of reading and expanded her reality. She lives a very quiet life and is a great support for me. I believe she is a wise woman and has been given the gift of prophecy. We communicate regularly, and she often expresses information about this time of change we are living in and always has wise words of support for me.

I went to visit my younger sister, Kathy, who was and still is very connected to Mother Earth. She lived on a farm, and I told her that a visitation happened, that an energy field went through my body, and that I had information in me about the time of change for humanity. I was overwhelmed and had no idea what was happening. I impulsively picked up a rock and put it in her hands. I did not think to do this, I just did it. Her fingers bent around the rock, and it was difficult to pry her fingers away from it. A transference of the energy happened, and she could feel the pulsating vibration right through her physical body. She said, "Don't be afraid, Sue. This is a gift, and it is good." Kathy is now doing fantastic work with the environment. She is teaching children and adults how to connect to Mother Earth. I acknowledge now that the stones on Mother Earth are like the bones in us. They hold vibration and memory.

From my sister Kathy's experience, I wondered if rocks could hold a vibration. I have a friend who travels somewhere different each year. I shared with her what was happening to me, yet she did not appear to physically connect to the vibrational energy. We came up with the idea of taking the vibration out into the world through the rocks. I collect rocks, hold them, bless them by saying a prayer on them, and then I give them to my friend to take with her on her travels. All over the world, she has deposited them whenever she feels the need to "put a rock down." Over the years, she has kept a map of where she has placed them all over Mother Earth. She has often said, "I don't even know why I'm doing this, yet I always get the feeling when to put a rock down." We laugh as we wonder whether this is actually doing anything, but every year she comes to collect the rocks!

My middle sister, Judy, was also activated and struggled with it. On her journey of transformation, she has often said, "It's like you don't have a choice; you're forced to go through the journey of change. You don't wake up one morning and say, 'Yes, I would love to now expand my reality.' With the activation, your life goes into a process of physical, mental, and emotional change. You can't stop it. It just is." She is a great healer, and I feel she is here to help children.

The magnetic energy force that penetrated my body was so strong that my whole nervous system was affected. I went into shock. I had no idea what had happened and can only now put it into words. I was not involved in any New Age thinking or searching for the meaning of life. I love my family, my home, my work, and my friends. I love the small, country lifestyle. I had absolutely no desire to change my life or look at the existence of humanity. I did not want this gift, and I hated it.

It was bazaar for ordinary people from the country like me and the other women. We often cry and laugh together. Mentally, I was in a state of shock, making it impossible to function on a daily level. I went to visit my father and brother, whom I looked upon as the two most logical people I knew. I figured they could either get rid of this or make some sense of it. I trusted them. I told them the world was going to go through big changes and it would affect them. They looked at me in disbelief, yet they were concerned about me, as I was crying and in an anxious state.

After they calmed me down, they said I was having a breakdown and told me to go to our holiday house for some rest. One morning while reading the newspaper, I had my right hand flat on the page of the newspaper, and my hand started shaking and touched three words on different parts of the paper. The three words were "You will understand." I knew that this was something beyond anyone's understanding, and it was proof to me that I wasn't having a breakdown. Something extraordinary had happened to me. I was still in state of fear, and I still didn't understand, yet this helped me know something bigger than my understanding was happening.

Information and automatic writing became a daily experience. I spent many days and evenings doing writings, which I started calling dotting because both hands would go to different words on a page. I would ask a question, and my hands would move to the index page of a book to what chapter I needed to go to. Then I would go to the chapter and allow my hands to find words that put a message together. If I needed a different page of the chapter, I would just feel this inside of me. I was asking questions about what was happening to us, and one of the first messages I received was "Thank you for allowing entry onto your planet. I am you, you are me, and we are one." I'm still not sure of what I've allowed entry to. The most challenging part of this process was I did not believe one word I wrote in the beginning because it was information I had never heard of. I would tell myself, "If you believe any of it, you will go mad."

I experienced profound insights into humanity's existence. We are at a crossroad in our evolution, and the heart is the access point for the next stage of our evolution. We have a bigger picture to our existence, as we separated from it eons ago. I always had a great love of God and people, and all the knowing inside of me could feel the structures of our human reality—such as financial, environment, social, and health structures—in a process of great change. The information deep inside me started to become a part of me as an all-encompassing knowing. It felt like the information was from another world and time and from a source outside of me. One day I was living what I perceived to be the safety of the world I had always known, and then I was experiencing a knowing that was totally opposite to the reality of human conditioning. I felt I was going insane. I lost all affinity with my family. I felt so isolated and lived in a world that was now only a memory to me. I felt alienated within my own family.

I was in overload and focused on what was happening to me and not on my business. My business went into bankruptcy. This was around six months after my experience with Anton. I felt a strong pull to move to Adelaide, and my husband, Wally, started looking for work in Adelaide. Before long, he got a job. With that, my family and I moved to Adelaide, and we endeavoured to make a new start. The small group of family and friends that I left behind kept in touch and gave much needed emotional support. I felt like I was losing control of my mind, and my free will had been taken over by someone or something. I was lost in this nightmare for months. During this time, my existence was in a state of retreating within, a feeling of being pulled or sucked into myself. I find this concept difficult to explain. I had no control over the experience. I felt encompassed by a feeling of going deeper and deeper into myself. This was a time in my journey where my physical world and my external reality were in a state of total nothingness. I had gone from being a very active woman, running my family and my business and being involved with community events, to a woman who found it difficult to function in daily life.

Not long after we all moved to Adelaide, the company that Wally worked for went into receivership, so he lost his job. We already were in a place of overwhelm and fear, and this didn't help. Due to the vibration happening in my body, I wasn't balanced enough to work. With this loss of his job and all that we had gone through, Wally lost purpose and direction, and we were on unemployment benefits for two years. Looking back at this time, it was really tough, but having Wally not work was better for me and the children. The youngest was four, and he thought of Wally as his playmate! Our eldest child, who was sixteen at the time, was the one that looked after all us, including leaving school and getting a job. Even though it was one of the worst times in all our lives, it felt good that we were all together and kept strong as a family unit.

During this time, I felt like I was being pulled down. I called them gravity days, as I could feel this heaviness in my physical body. I could feel a buzzing feeling in my temples. I was not sleeping well and often had this amnesia feeling. I felt like I was dying. I cried a lot and yelled at God, as I felt a part of me was leaving. I was not depressed, as this was a process of feeling overwhelmed, and I had no information available to me to understand what was happening. What I was living through was a dying, the letting go of my old beliefs and conditions. My whole nervous system was on overload, and I found it physically difficult to drive a car or walk to school to collect our son. Terror controlled my inner self. I was in spiritual crisis but did not know it at the time.

Kay came to visited me in Adelaide, and as we opened a bottle of wine, she acknowledged me for my strength and courage. She said, "I've watched this vibration nearly kill you. It was too much for your physical being to integrate." Before my activation, I was living in a body and a reality with an energy field at a level of five, and then with the electromagnetic force field, it accelerated to fifty. This is a demonstration of what it felt like to instantly go from one reality to another. I now know that the three years during which my external world did not move were the hardest work I will ever have to endure in my entire life. I had to hang on so tightly to my sanity. A rapid change of consciousness was in progress, an integration of a magnetic force field into my physical body. I was infused with a blueprint through a portal that had opened up on Mother Earth. This portal was a place of triggering light codes where the nervous system was able to take on electrical currents into the body. This is something new that was born, and it was a new light frequency. It was like putting your foot into a shoe that didn't fit, and no one around me could see that I had left my previous existence.

There were times when the outside world repulsed me. I felt it was poisoning me, and at times I found it difficult to breathe. I could see the lies and illusions of our human existence so clearly. No one around me could see that I was remembering other times and places of human evolution. There were times when I did not know how I was going to endure the process. What to think and what to believe was a nightmare for me. My whole world was changing, and I had left the reality my family was in. The pain in me was immense. I had always been a mother who was there for her children. It was very difficult for me to be a part of their lives because of the process that was happening to me. It was taking me away from their beliefs, and I had been a part of teaching these beliefs.

My husband found it very difficult, as he had no idea what was happening to me, and he became objective and afraid. As things happened to me, I shared them with him, as he was my best friend. I told him about this knowing in me, about a time of great changes on our planet. I would say to him, "I feel that many of our structures are in a process of change, and I am concerned for our family. This world is created from illusions, and nothing is based on truth. The lies will surface in our lifetime." He would just look at me, and even though he would not make me wrong, we could not talk about it, as we were both living in different realities. I shared with him about the money markets globally in chaos and that superannuation was not going to be there for many people, that the housing markets were going to fall, and the environmental issues were going to create weather pattern changes. I told him all this twenty-five years ago.

My whole nervous system was affected, and this made it hard for me to function. My husband was very concerned about what was happening. At the time, he just wanted the old me back. We became distant from each other, and he asked me to "please let this all go." I had to first come to some acceptance myself, and I remember saying to him very strongly, "I feel we are becoming strangers. It's not me that has to accept this; it is you, for this is bigger than our marriage. I can't stop this."

There was no one for me to talk to. I lived in silence in the process and felt very alone. My only communication was with my friends in my country town. I knew if I was to seek medical advice with what I was experiencing, they would have sedated me and labelled me as suffering from a mental condition. The alternative healers I went to had no awareness of what was happening to me. They said I must be channelling from another source, but I felt I wasn't. It felt different. I went to some New Age bookshops and started to read books, trying to find some answers. The thinking that prevailed in these books was that I was responsible for my own thoughts; I could change them and take control of my life. This had been my personal reality before my experience, yet what was happening to me was totally opposite.

My own thoughts were fighting for survival. How I understood life and what I believed to be my truth about who I was—I felt like something had taken over these beliefs. I felt my choice and free will were being interfered with. I felt like what I wanted for myself and for my family no longer mattered. I had no choice. I could have been the most positive person with the strongest intent of thought about what I wanted to achieve, but something bigger was happening inside of me. I wanted one thing, and the force field wanted another. I was at war inside of myself. My thoughts were around evolution, the massive changes for humanity, the magnetic grid lines, and Mother Earth. I was consciously thinking these thoughts. I did not want them, I did not understand them, and I wanted my old life back and my old thoughts.

I remember saying to my husband, "I am going insane. I need help, and I want you to take me to a place where you can get help for mental issues."

He said, "I can't do that because I feel like I would be betraying you." So he decided to take me to my aunt's for her advice, as he trusted her. I agreed, as I thought if I told her, she would take me to the medical system for help. However, she suggested I see her minister first. I thought the minister would think that some negative force had hold of me. The minister came, and we talked for several hours, and at the end of the conversation, this man gave me the strength to keep going.

He said, "I have only known you for a few hours, Susan, and you are not insane. Something has happened to you that is unexplainable from the way we understand life, and your own will is fighting it."

Then he said, "Susan, let go and let God." I have learnt in my journey that the right people come along at the right time. This was a critical time for me, and the minster's advice gave me hope and strength.

My mother did the same for me. Even though she was very religious, she was also a very open person for her age. She had a great faith in God, and she worried about me. She would often say, "I think God has asked too much of you, Susan."

On my journey, I have always been taken care of. At my lowest moment, someone has always been there. I could not stop what was happening to me in my daily process of inner change. The beliefs I was born into were being forced to leave me. In time, I came to an acceptance, and I became mentally, emotionally, and physically stronger. The shock and feelings of overwhelm were leaving me, and I was slowly integrating the force field into my own energy field. I did not understand this at the time, and I consciously had no understanding of the information that was rising in me about human evolution and our separation. These thoughts were not mine. I was not hearing voices, yet I could felt an incredible knowing. It was stronger than any belief I had ever experienced, as the information was inside of me, not outside.

I was not channelling; I was experiencing this amazing knowing from within myself.

My ability to function in my everyday life improved, and I was able to live normally in my environment. My physical body was adjusting to the magnetic energy force field, and my mental and emotional states were regaining balance. As we needed to live life and pay the rent and the daily bills, I knew that either Wally or I needed to go back to work. A friend who worked in a care facility for the elderly asked if I had some spare time, as they needed kitchen staff. I said yes and began work there.

The first person outside of my family and friends that I confided in about my experience was a nurse in my new workplace. You meet people that are like minded, and you can share with these people about what you are experiencing. They will say something in conversation, and then you know they think differently from others, and you have a connection with these people. He gave me the love and support to tell him about what had happened to me. He encouraged me to write and to know that what had happened was not to be feared.

Two other ladies from the nursing home gave me love and support to accept what was happening to me. One of the girls told me to go outside each night, put my hands out, and say, "I accept." I did this for about six months, and this process helped me to let go and accept. Prior to this, I was clenching my fists and expressing my anger. I needed to let this experience happen and go with it and not hold it within. I began to surrender to what was happening to me, and I had stabilised enough to be normal in my daily life. Most people did not know of the transformation that was taking place in me, as I kept silent about it with most people that came into my daily life. It was like I was living in two worlds.

I felt like I was dying, and Mother Earth was going through a natural process of evolution. Humanity is going to go through a time of transformation. My love for my children was the driving force that gave me enough strength and purpose to live through each day. The dying feeling I experienced was the letting go of a world that I had once loved and understood. I could feel the game of separation everywhere, and this made everything that I knew about God and social beliefs covered in illusions. I fought so hard to hang on to the old beliefs. I did not easily accept the process that was happening to me, and I often stated how I hated it. I argued and yelled at the process. I became adept at swearing, and I cried a lot. I did not want the knowing or the insights. I wanted my family and my old world back. The old thoughts and beliefs were struggling for survival.

I was having thoughts of the history that humanity currently knows of as the only timeframe reference of our existence. I was beginning to understand that there are times, places, and people that exist and that are not a part of this present history. I had a knowing that our systems that have provided us with structures and a way of life and that have separated and divided humanity are in a time of completion. Our beliefs about God and light were about separation and control while the truth was coming up deeply from the very core of my being. The knowing grew so strong that my thoughts, the way I saw things, and my beliefs, were forced to remain still and to surrender to the process.

I came to a place of acceptance, and finally the war within me subsided. I just could not fight the knowing anymore, and I gradually started to trust myself. I knew what was happening to me was from inside me and not from someone or something separate or outside of me. I keep silent about this for many years because the information from most New Age books and teachers was that we were channelling information from other beings to help the transformation of humanity. Whenever I told my story, it was assumed that Anton was giving me information. This did not happen, as his communication was "I am here to give you transformation for humanity. I am not your teacher." I never communicated to Anton other than the first interaction. The knowing, the wisdom, and the healing were a part of me, and it's a part of everyone. I was not channelling from another being; I had simply returned to the truth of myself, and this is a natural process for all of humanity.

The being, Anton, was the gatekeeper of an ancient temple, originating from an ancient race and from another dimension. It has taken me many years of acceptance and allowing my knowing to have a place of respect and honour and to stop my self-doubt. It's like I was living in the world but not of this world. Slowly I started to trust my writing and dotting. Dotting, as I mentioned, is what I call it when I put my hand on the index page of a book, ask where I need to go, and my fingers just go to the right words and make a sentence. This is so normal for me now twenty-five years later. I laugh about it now as my own worth has grown. I believed it when my dotting said that my heart of love was like a magnetic force field and had been pulled to this site at Horsnell Gully, the sacred site that I connected to. Anton triggered the sacred details of the pre-ordained patterning of a new code of reality within me and released the order of separation and connected me to full activation of the connection with Mother Earth. There is no separation, and the memory of our human existence is still in the rocks of Mother Earth. The Earth's frequency is a very powerful force field and is activated within me. The knowledge and knowing of all that is, this is in all of us.

I began to understand that I had lived a life not knowing who I was. I believed in a reality that had control over human existence. In the old story, I had accepted what I was told about creation, power, money, love, self-worth, wisdom, and God. I was now experiencing this control leaving me. I had always been disconnected from the true power source within myself through my own separation.

I went on a journey of transformation and let go of the doubts and pain around my own experience of activation. Why this happened to me was a question I often asked. On my journey, I met people who had a theory that I chose to do this before I was born. My jovial response to this theory was that if I chose to go through this exchange of realities in such a way, I must have been under the influence of alcohol or pushed when I agreed!

When great change happens in our lives, we often go on a search for information and understanding. It was time for me to remember who I was. With my interaction with Anton, I went to a place of ancient tribal people, a place where the ancient wisdom under the Earth was open to me. The secrets of this place of origin were to be accessed for me to open and walk through this doorway. This will affect the collective consciousness of humanity as many people in different places living on Earth have agreed to help awaken and activate the memory of humanity. There is a mission in place. We have a common goal of unshakable commitment and integrity. The pre-encoded memories will reawaken.

At Horsnell Gully, I entered an amazing, powerful vortex that was connected to an ancient civilisation on Earth before our recorded history, a civilisation with a more advanced consciousness and a higher frequency. The vortex gave me direct alignment with the higher pulsating frequency. The correspondence that was activated within me was like molecules of a new grid, understanding a higher truth and embodied in love. Upon interaction with the being, Anton, I opened a doorway to a magnetic intervention to help transform human consciousness. Humanity will move from their sleep and activate on a scale never before experienced. A spiral of evolution will release under a time-frame mechanism, a frequency from Mother Earth. An electromagnetic energy force will reveal a place of origin calling us to go home, calling us to remember the vibrational frequency. A higher order of love is our heritage.

The journey to accept this information has been extraordinary. I have no scientific evidence, no proof, just an unshakable commitment in my evolution for the purpose of serving humanity's evolution. We are at a time of evolutionary change, and there will be intense periods of global restructuring. We are blessed to have accepted passing through human conditioning. This will give us many opportunities to create a different world.

I have met some amazing people on my journey, people from all walks of life. They are pioneers to a new way of understanding and experiencing life. I often felt that most of the population were having a party, having no realisation or understanding of the people going through massive transformation, receiving access to new knowledge and healing, and being introduced to a new world. Their experience was mental, emotional, physical, and spiritual.

When I look back over the last twenty-five years, I can see that the most difficult part of the journey was not living in the same reality as my family. I have seen others experience the same when husbands, wives, partners, children, sisters, brothers, and parents think the person is going insane. Many relationships do not deal well with this process. This experience is about individual evolution being bigger than any relationship structure.

My journey put a great deal of pressure on my husband and me. We existed in two different worlds for many years. We needed to go through many changes to accept and come to terms with all of this. There were times when we both felt overwhelmed and confused, and I felt I had lost my best friend. Our communication was always there, and I did speak to him about many of the things that were presenting themselves to me. I would wake up at night, groaning in emotional pain, and tell him this pain was not just mine, it was part of the pain of the denial of the feminine on the planet. He would just look at me and eventually learned to accept that this was how it was for me. Our commitment to our family was and still is absolute. Even though this was our driving force, I know he worried about where this was all going to take me.

My experience changed my children's lives. My love for them was my driving force to keep going forward and to live through each day. My daughter, Heidi, was fifteen at the time of my activation, and leaving her country town was very painful. She had great anger and resistance to my transformation and activation. I was very connected to her and then suddenly not connected to her, as our realities were in two different worlds. The old world died in me, and we became poles apart. It was really painful for her, as she wanted her old mum back. It has taken her many years to come to a place of acceptance. I remember my sisters saying, "Keep the door open, keep the loving going, and she will come back," and she has. She now has her own children, and we have a great relationship. On her wedding day, she wrote the most beautiful letter thanking me and telling me what an amazing mother I have been. It was an amazing healing for both of us. From the time of the activation in me until Heidi was sixteen, I tried the best I could to keep my transformation process away from my children. I told them that we were living in amazing times, although sometimes in the beginning I communicated fear about the time of change, because I was in fear for them.

My son Luke was fourteen when we arrived in Adelaide. He had such strong dreams to be a world-level golfer, so going to the city added to his dreams. Luke and I would talk a lot, as he was open to the communication, and I would tell him some of the things I was going through. Luke was a big dreamer and wanted to achieve a lot. He was so focused on in his own dream that my process and transformation didn't affect him like it affected his sister. I don't think he lost the connection to me like Heidi did. He was happy to be in Adelaide and has achieved a lot. He is still a man of great dreams. He now has children of his own and has told me that he hopes he can share the wisdom that I gave him to his children.

My other son, Jed, was three when my activation happened. When we arrived in Adelaide, Jed was a bubble of love, and we all gravitated towards him. As we were all going through our own experiences of accepting living in the city, he was the glue that kept us together. He only knew me as the activated person and would wake up most mornings hearing me speak into my Dictaphone. He thought it was normal that his mum did this! The information was normal to him. He felt lucky that I was his mum, and I felt he already knew the information and that he was born with it.

My children have their own stories about this time that changed our lives. From the activations and then shifting to Adelaide and living out their lives with a mum who thinks a little different.

Wally and I are not on the same page, yet we are in the same book. Our commitment to our family has walked the journey through the time of my activation. I feel blessed to have my family, and it has provided me with stability, purpose, and love. It always gave me a place to be. Wally is a great man and has always made me laugh. His humour often saved the day for all of us.

Insights, knowledge, and healing are often part of one's journey as you walk forward. At the beginning, twenty-five years ago, there were no words to describe my experience. As I walked forward in my evolution, new words opened up to me. As my worth and belief grew, my acceptance expanded. People, places, and things came my way to pave pathways for my growth. A healing modality called rebirthing/breath work is a breathing technique that may assist a person in seeing thought patterns and behaviours in their past that may prevent them from living a life fully in the present. I have a great love and respect for rebirthing, as it provided me a safe space to let go and heal the resistance in me. It provided answers to me that were hiding in my own consciousness.

I decided to do the rebirther training with the Australian Academy of Rebirthing\Breathwork, and in experiencing a warm-water rebirth, which is a very powerful process, I found answers to the question I had often asked. A warm-water rebirth eases and relaxes you. The body has many holding patterns and trapped memories, and this is built into the muscular structure of the body. In the warm-water rebirth experience, it felt like the water was speaking to my body, saying, "Life is safe," and it helped me see the truth. I felt that I had never been asked permission for the activation to take place, and I battled with that, as I felt that I had no choice. Many spiritual people around me would tell me this is not how it works and that I did give my permission, but I felt strongly that this was not so.

My experience of the rebirth was that every time I went to put on the snorkel mask, I would lose my breath. After many attempts, I eventually became determined and put the mask on, and with all my strength, I kept my face under water. I started to feel myself moving and going towards a light, and I sensed a presence that said, "You need to take this information and go back."

At Jed's birth, my youngest child, I had an emergency caesarean. My other two were natural births. During Jed's birth, I almost died. The rebirth showed me and provided me with insight into Jed's birth, which was connected to the activation, especially around my issue of not being asked permission. At home after the rebirth, I started dotting, and the message said, "At the operating table, you met the being and made an agreement." I don't know if this being was Anton or another being. It blew my mind, as I was starting to believe the messages, and I was too scared to keep dotting in case I found out deeper information that I wasn't ready for. I believe nothing is a coincidence in our lives, and everything is in its right place and order. Yet, there is so much we do not understand. It is like when you are ready, the teacher will arrive, healing the pain, beliefs, and conditions that are stopping you from being all that you can be and are interfering with the purpose you have come here to fulfil, which is a part of the transformation that is experienced.

For me, another modality that I totally resonate with and that has provided great healing for me and my family is Family Constellations, which I studied in Brisbane, Australia. This technique is about putting the order of love back in its right place in family, working with past generations and energy that is influencing us in our present day, in our relationship with ourselves, our partners, family, money, health, work, and purpose. This work has given me insight and has healed my self-worth, power, and beliefs about myself. It provided me with the ability to fully love and see the magnificence in both my parents before they died. It has given me the opportunity to take life fully as life was passed on to me through my parents. I presently use this technique in my work, which provides opportunities for clients to let go of the old story that lives in them and to walk into the new story that is birthing for humanity.

A little over ten years ago, when I wrote the book called *An Ordinary Woman's Extraordinary Journey*, I wanted to rid myself of this information. I wrote the book to get the information out of me so I could move on with my life. I didn't want to have anything to do with it once the book was printed. I was scared of being exposed and hoped the book would just hide under the bed. People would ask me how they could get a copy of the book, and I would put my hand over my mouth and mumble because I really didn't want them to buy the book. I was embarrassed and felt vulnerable.

At the time, I was back to living an ordinary life working as Diversional Therapist at the age care facility, and most people that knew me had no idea that I had thoughts like I did. I hid from it, and even though I loved my work with the aged, I felt the nursing home was a nice place for me to hide. It took a great deal of courage for me to write the book and to stand up and speak at the book launch. My whole family was there, and I was concerned for my children. I was worried about what their friends might think. Heidi said, "Mum, don't worry. I'll tell them your home from Glenside because Dad misses you." (Glenside was a hospital for people with mental health issues.) I now know it was not the right time, as I was not ready to stand in my truth. I was saying things like the heart is our power source, the next stage of evolution is not a thought process, and the access is in the human heart, and most people found it difficult to understand this information. It felt that I was being asked to pull this vibration down to humanity, and it was difficult, for the vibration did not have words. It was an energy frequency.

I have met many people who are being pulled into many different areas of work to help anchor the expansion of consciousness. They are financial advisors, doctors, nurses, petrol station managers, school teachers, healers, child care workers, age care workers, mothers, fathers, sons, and daughters, clearing practitioners, rebirthing practitioners, Family Constellation practitioners, and other healing modalities. I am amazed where people are being placed to make a difference.

I have now spent the last decade with full commitment to accept and understand what happened to me. In her later years, my mother always said to me, "You have to do this work, or you'll never be content." When the girls who were activated and I got together over a drink, we would often say, "God, haven't we done a bloody good job to survive this?" We came to realise that we must have agreed to experience this frightening time together as a group.

I would like to acknowledge the amazing journey that many of our pioneers have been on. Great courage and strength has been needed. Many people have walked alone with a pull inside causing them to look at life in a new way. Many had phenomenal experiences while receiving this information and knowledge about the human race, and these experiences are not understood or accepted in our present world. We are living in an amazing time of change, and the structures in place do not have the information or understanding to educate people about this natural process of human evolution. Many do not believe this information, but through a daily life of change, it will take them there. Millions will go through the process freely as the pioneers have opened a doorway for humanity to walk through. Millions will be forced to change. This change is not to be feared; it is to be understood as a natural part of our evolution.

Pioneers of Today

*Heart calling to you to
announce the return of your heritage.
You are complete,
now able to enter
the mystery and
observe your earthly history,
finally discovering your highest truth.
What a battle you have fought
to reach this time of completion.*

2

Pioneers of Today

The winds of change are calling. We can feel it everywhere. Life feels like it is on the run. Time is always knocking at our door, and it seems like there is a quickening happening. It is hard to keep up all the time, and often it feels like time is running out. Even our children talk about it, as life is on the run for them too. Children always live as if a day is a long time, and it seems to take a long time to go from childhood to adulthood. Now it comes so quickly. Calendar events, Christmas, birthdays, anniversaries, they all feel like they come around each year so much faster than before. Life is so fast. It is like we are on a train that is moving with extraordinary speed, and feelings of confusion and being out of control are often spoken about. As we view the world globally, we can see that structures, such as financial, environmental, social, political, educational, health, law, science, and religious structure, are in a place of change. Fear is often in us, as these structures have provided us with stability and progress.

The year 2012 had many predictions and prophesies around it. Books were written about it, including ancient writings. Tribal people and the mystics who are connected to Mother Earth speak of an amazing time of change for humanity around this time and date. Change is a natural part of life; it is like the breath that is always there. As we look back in history, we will see the changes that have created the present world we live in. Change has always been a part of us—being born and going through the natural processes of childhood, adolescent, adulthood, and then aging and dying. Century after century, we have been birthing new ideas around ways to live life. So why is the year 2012 and beyond, and the talk about change, so different from the changes of our past history?

The ancient writings, such as those of the Mayans, speak of massive changes never experienced before in our history. They speak of humanity being at a crossroad of destruction and needing to take on a new spiritual understanding about themselves. Prophesies from great visionaries like Edgar Cayce talk about these times with great detail. Doom and gloom have often been felt by the way we have read and understood many of the great prophesies. Some New Age thinkers talk of gloom, as they have indicated catastrophic earth changes, pole shifts, and only a few surviving this time. There are many books that have been written about this time we are living in, about the expansion and positive impact on the human race. For example, *Fractal Time*, *The God Code*, *The Divine Matrix*, and *The Secret of 2012 and a New World Age* were written by bestselling author Gregg Braden. Others are 2013: *End of Days or a New Beginning—Envisioning the World after the Events of 2012*, written by Marie D. Jones, author Neale Donald Walsch's *Conversations with God*, and Barbara Marx Hubbard's *Birth 2012 and Beyond*.

From the perspective of an ordinary woman without any university education or studies in science or religion, experiencing a phenomena that changed my life and opened me to a new reality of human existence, my message is about what an amazing time we are living in. The creation of a new story for humanity, a time when we will open up to a bigger picture of who we are. This time will provide us with many new opportunities to grow and manifest a new vision for our world.

The times we are living through include massive changes, and it is very important that we have information and education about this time of change. The most difficult part of this is that the information and education are not available from our present structures. There is no information in our present human reality of intellect about this next stage of human evolution taking place. There is no evidence or fact in our scientific world that makes this next stage of our evolution real. So the mass population globally has no awareness or acceptance of a new story being created for humanity, a story of connection and wholeness and a new way of experiencing life.

Humanity is at a time of ending, and the feeling of time running out is real. This end is the completion of the way we have lived and understood life; it is the end of an old story of humanity, of disconnection, separation, and division. All of us globally, whether we have an understanding of it or not, are living in an incredible time of our human existence. A birth of a new humanity. Wow, what a time to be living, as this birth is a new beginning and a new story of who we are.

Gloom and doom, destruction, and fear can be a daily reality for many if they do not understand what is happening in our world, as many of the old structures of stability and progress are changing globally. Confusion and instability do not need to be the driving force of reality during this time of change. We are evolving globally in this time of completion and the birth of interconnectedness. There is a journey that humanity is being asked to take, and you may ask who is doing the asking. There is so much more to us than the five senses we have used to experience life. We have amazing sciences that have provided us with knowledge about the physical, mental, and emotional parts of ourselves. What we accept as our truth is always in a place of continual change as research and science bring forward new findings.

What I experienced twenty-five years ago I know was science, yet it is beyond the science of today. It was an experience of expanded consciousness taking me to places inside of me that I had never heard of, a higher self, divinity of self, and a very deep place that I did not know existed. Some people call it soul communication. What I know is that this greater part is in all humanity but not visible or accepted as being needed as part of our daily life. This higher aspect of us is not in our thinking or intellect or our reality. The masses globally do not know it exists, and I didn't either. I had a love of God, and that was it. Many do not have knowledge or any awareness of this greater part of us, so this time we are living in will provide us with opportunities to see life in a new way. We will be exposed to new ideas about universal worlds, and we will be asked to expand many of our current beliefs and let go of many old conditions. This time is about change and can be experienced with growth and gratitude, as an expansion of us is the driving force of such an amazing time to witness.

To have a place of acceptance and willingness to change and open to new ways is a journey that few have accepted. They are the pioneers of our time, ordinary people who have heard and felt the winds of change inside of them. Very often in our history, it has taken ordinary men, women, and children to bring about great change and insights for the good of all humankind.

We once believed our world was flat, and you could fall off it. We had no knowledge of gravity or the circumference of the globe. It took pioneers of the day great courage and commitment to bring about new information and realisations that provided new ways of looking at and experiencing life. Pioneers of the day have always been a driving force behind the great changes of civilisation, and they have needed to stand up with beliefs that are different from the mainstream thinking. This has been very challenging, and many people have been persecuted for doing this.

There are new pioneers of today opening to new information about who we are. A bigger picture is being exposed to them. These pioneers are people who have listened and felt the call to change, and they could be your neighbour, your mother, your father, your sister, your brother, your friends, your work colleagues, ordinary people viewing and experiencing life differently.

A small percentage of the population of the globe has been experiencing something amazing, new, and different. The other larger population has no idea or understanding of the journey of the pioneers of today. Great acknowledgment is needed here for the pioneers of our day, as they have been working with full commitment, strength, and courage for many years. These pioneers have opened up information for our health and well-being and often have been challenged by the mainstream authority. These are new ideas, such as we are not victims to diseases, and illnesses can be created from discord within ourselves through mental, emotional, physical, and spiritual imbalance. Some are providing evidence that depression is connected to the deep sadness about the disconnection inside of us and not truly knowing and loving ourselves. There are many new theories being born, and all have the aspect of the spiritual part of us playing a major role in our health and well-being, a new way of life.

Many pioneers are standing up about social change, knowing that we are all connected. The starvation of our babies and children on this planet needs to stop, and we have the capacity to do this if we look at life differently. Climate change has been a big one for many pioneers in bringing about information and new realisations that something is in the process of change on our planet. This has needed great commitment. Then there is the natural process of a deep change calling for ordinary men and women. This is difficult to explain, as there is something big happening. There are teachers and leaders who have come on the planet to educate and provide some understanding about the time we are living in. These people often have no proof or scientific evidence to back their beliefs up, yet they hold great intention, commitment, and courage for their purpose of service for humanity because the information, the knowledge, and knowing is inside them.

The pioneers of today have opened a doorway for humanity to walk through. This doorway was closed, and to open it, ordinary people have been on a journey of their own individual evolution. It has been extraordinary. These pioneers were asked to pierce the boundaries of human thought, human reality, and walk through human conditioning and beliefs. Penetrating the boundary of human reality can be frightening with no information, no rules, or plans in place. These people were asked to open the doorway that has kept humanity in prison. There has been great preparation on Mother Earth for this time of completion of the old story and birth of the new story. It feels like there is a bigger plan in place.

When going through a time of transformation or giving up the old ways of thinking, some pioneers have experienced feelings of instability, feelings of insanity, delusional connection to the past and confusing it with the present. This happened to me, and I have seen it happen to many of my friends going through what is called the shift of consciousness. I have read many healing books through my journey of change and while training in the field of my profession, rebirthing, and Family Constellations. The information in the books talks about the journey of transformation and change—the mental, emotional, physical, and spiritual rollercoaster of change, insights, growth, and healing. I also have clients that experience symptoms as they let go of the old ways, and some speak of a feeling like madness and how it was very painful needing all of their strength and courage to live through the journey. Some of the pioneers experienced many days when they felt they were living in two worlds, the one world that their family and friends lived in and this new world that started to open to the pioneers. The two worlds were often in opposition to each other, and at times they felt they were on their hands and knees, not knowing where to go next. There were days when they wanted to get off the journey of expansion that was happening to them. Yet try as they may, it was impossible because they had heard the call of change inside of them. Something big was taking place. Some have left relationships and careers because they found it too difficult to evolve with the restrictions from old conditions.

Their commitment has been in faith, a natural knowing being exposed to them, a feeling of opening to something new and often not being able to name it. Their mental body often felt fatigue in the process of seeing, understanding, and letting go of old beliefs. The emotional body often yelled out loudly its confusion, and madness would show strongly for many pioneers on the journey of change. Yet the pull, the calling continued. Often their own thoughts could not believe they would be willing to participate in this process of letting go of so much of their conditioning that was their old truth. It often left them in a place of grief, as the old ways and old beliefs were what they had known and loved, and now they were letting them go. Their own thoughts did not understand; they could argue as much as they wanted to, but it would not stop the calling of expansion. What was happening to the pioneers was not a personal choice, not an intellectual decision, and many days they wanted to pull the plug to stop the change. The calling just got stronger, and trust and intuition became the guiding light for daily life.

This is all happening to many of the pioneers while they are trying to live life in mainstream reality with family, friends, work, and community. The majority of the people around them have no idea what is taking place for many of the pioneers. They need all of their inner strength and courage to live this way and often are judged for seeing new ways of looking at life. The call came to many over the last few decades. All of them were asked to hear their own heart stories. The pain went deep, going through conditioning, beliefs, finding the lack of worth, no love for the self, healing the pain of many generations, and some experienced past lives. The deep healing has taken place globally. If you have spent time at workshops and conferences involved in healing work or looking at life in a new way through different healing modalities, you have heard and seen many pioneers opening their heart. Their heart has cried out to them, and they have realised what they came to Mother Earth to do, to open their heart and free it from the lies and illusions that have been a way of life for all of us. Their own self-doubt would spoke loudly in judgment of this inner pull. Their physical body felt the vibrational change as they released the abuse, denial, and numbness that would often manifest as body ailments. When energy in the body is blocked, disease and decay are often the outcome. Many healed the pain from past generations as it was passed on to them. The ways of devaluation of each other cannot come through to us to be a part of the new story, so all must be healed. Some people have put their hand up (so to speak) to do this for many. As there is no separation, this is what happens when you heal the devaluation in your life; you heal it for many others too.

The pioneers are now remembering the ancient writings that were lost, as these memories are inside of them. They are connecting and communicating to galactic worlds, and some are entering the sacred geometry of Mother Earth. All are providing knowledge and information about the bigger picture.

The pioneers are creating new businesses that hold the space and provide information and techniques for people going through the shift of consciousness and to help this natural process of evolution take place with ease. Businesses such as reiki, rebirthing, Family Constellations, cranio sacral therapy, quantum therapists, intuitive mediums, crystal healing, Tibetan bowls, and many more. Energy work is available for the physical body to help us align with the natural process, to experience emotional release from the rollercoaster ride that can take place, easing anxiety, depression, and grief. Confusion often keeps us company as we walk the road to freeing ourselves from any belief or pattern that has kept us from being all we can be. When you have let go of the old way of doing life, you get a spring in your step as you feel lighter and free and see life in a new way. There are sacred spaces in the new businesses for the heart stories to be told, expressed, and let go of, as the pain is part of the old story of creation.

The year 2012 was a timeframe for the pioneers. It is important that we understand what we have done in our time of healing and letting go of the lies and illusion. We have amazing strength to hear the call. What we have done in this time is heal ourselves, as well as many others, and open the doorway that humanity has lived behind. We have been like the midwives waiting for a new birth, and now we are at this time. The doorway is fully opened.

New leaders are needed to stand and lead humanity through the doorway. These new leaders will come from all walks of life and often come from places the intellect would not view as leaders. They will not lead as the leaders of our present system, as that leadership is from the old story and the old structure. New leaders will be standing in a new truth, having the ability to hear their own heartbeat and hear humanity's heartbeat, letting go of the old stories and the old ways we are familiar with. What is happening on Mother Earth is a vibrational change. The old structures were created from a race of people that did not know who they were. This statement about the masses will sound to most people "out there," odd, and unreal. The political, social, economic, law, education, health, and religious structures were all created from beliefs and conditions of the old ways. We were not connected, we lived separated, and we believed in the old story of disconnection. What was created was the belief of a reality of deception, control, and manipulation, part of the old way, the old story of human creation.

The new leaders have taken back the lost knowledge, wisdom, and truth and provided humanity with a bigger picture of who they are, therefore giving a deeper understanding of the old world that is in a time of completion. In the transition time, our structures that have given us stability will be asked to expand to the new story of operating from a place of oneness and no separation. This is not being asked from human demand; it is being asked from evolution, and it is not easy to explain to people that are living in the energy of the old way, the energy of disconnection and separation. This is not to make someone wrong or less than someone who has heard the call of the pulsation from evolution. Humanity is totally innocent, for it has no knowledge of the separation of itself. The leaders will be asked to stand next to the mass population and walk with them, acknowledging that the mass population is also the impulse of evolution, all perfect and in its right order. The new leaders will help humanity take back and own its heritage.

Humanity's heritage has been forgotten, as it was taken away from us. We are the people of love and light, and it is our birth right to know the truth and the bigger picture of existence. Humanity has walked a long journey of human existence. It is all in our history books, and we have finally reached this time of completion. There are many stories about our creation, and science and religion are often in opposition. Our truth is bigger than both the science and religion of today, and this information was lost eons ago.

There is much more to us than our present belief and understanding has. We are at a time in evolution where the bigger picture will be exposed to us, and we have what it takes to take our heritage back. When we are born into a family, this becomes our family linage, our birth place and our country of origin. The ancestors from our family line, parents and grandparents, are all a part of our family heritage. We also have a larger family, and it is called humanity. We have a heritage that was taken from us, our natural blueprint, and we are a race of people without our true origin. We need to take our heritage back. We are a race of people who have reached a crossroad in the balance of life, and we need to stop living from the conditions of the present progress, materialism, and capitalism. The balance of life is being disrupted, and the present structures of our world do not have the answers to support this crossroad. This has taken us to a natural process of expansion. Taking our heritage back is an evolutionary journey, and it's on an evolutionary timeframe. It is about looking beyond the history of our history book, as the picture is enormous, and there is so much we do not understand about ourselves. It is about knowing that we are all connected, and this connection opens us up to a different communication. It is from an energy vibration, a magnetic force field that is able to take us into a different world of interaction with the galactic worlds and connection to Mother Earth. Taking our heritage back is not available from the reality of the information within our current structures. There is no way to work it out from our mind's perspective. It is from our evolutionary place in time, and our mind is not being asked to work it out. This can be confusing, as our mind has always worked life out for us, yet our mind will expand in this natural process that is taking place.

Within our DNA, there are codes of remembrance about the lost ancient writings, wisdom and truth, knowledge of the people of love and light, the separation that happened to them, and the invasion that changed them. It is time in our evolution for this memory to be activated. The activation to remember is not a thought process though. You can acquire information to provide an understanding of what is taking place on Mother Earth, yet the activation and remembrance are not available to you from this information. This is because the activation and remembrance are not a thought; the thinking gets in the way. The activation is an electromagnetic frequency activation.

We are a race of people who have not lived from our true origin. We are a part of the people of love and light. This may not mean a great deal to many people in their busy life schedules, living the belief and conditions of our productive world, just living life, growing up, getting an education, finding partners, having families, careers, keeping house, paying the bills, etc. Many people would be happy to leave the bigger picture up to science and religion. Ordinary people are doing the best they can and want the greatest life possible for themselves and their families. Some are happy to do personal development with the hope of a more productive life. Some have the knowledge that what we think is what we create. Even though all of this information will come with us to be a part of the new story, the picture is bigger. What is happening on Mother Earth is much bigger than the thoughts of humanity.

Most people are living life to provide for their needs to be met, and it is all that they are interested in. Keeping up with everyday life is challenging enough, and unless they can feel the pulsating pull of evolution inside of them, why would they question life and the bigger picture? Why would they even consider that there is a heritage they have forgotten and that there is a doorway opened for them to walk through to expose them to a new story of creation? They would say to this, "You are mad to even think any of this." I understand this because I thought just like most of the people in mainstream thinking, happy to be in their own present world with no exposure to a bigger picture. I would have been happy to stay in that old paradigm, as it was what I knew and loved. Yes, sometimes life was difficult in this old paradigm, yet somehow you found a way around it. Yes you saw bad things happening to good people, and sometimes you questioned why. But to consider a lost heritage, ancient writings, and connection to Mother Earth was ridiculous. And then evolution called me. It was on a timeframe, and my life changed. You do not need to be looking for a spiritual change in your life. Evolution has called humanity back home, and there will be a mass stirring, an activation of memory for masses of people on Mother Earth.

We have lived in our world without any true connection to Mother Earth. We have made decisions for the progress of our world without this connection. We have not had the information or knowledge about the interconnectedness to all things. The place of connection to Mother Earth is our heartbeat that operates from an electromagnetic force field that is a part of all there is. Yet we have not been able to understand this science. The human heart has an electromagnetic force field that extends out. It is much more powerful than our brain or thought processes. New sciences from our pioneer leaders, such as Gregg Braden and Bruce Lipton, in this evolution are bringing us facts about the power of our heart. Pioneer leaders like Joseph Chilton Pearce teach about the intelligence of the heart. It is the power source of creation; it is the place of connection and the next stage in our evolution. This information is being expressed from pioneers of our time who have opened up to a deep memory and who are getting this information from other dimensions and uncovering the ancient writings for the purpose of this time of completion of the old way of living and understanding the disconnection and separation of our old existence. In the birth of the new way of living, all things are connected, and we have ability to interact with other dimensions with a higher truth, from a place of connection. It is like you are living with a different electronic wave, like tuning into a specific radio frequency.

A natural order of balance is in place, and a pulsating vibrational frequency is being felt by many, linking them back to the connection of our Mother Earth. Her electromagnetic force field is activated, and we are a part of the magnetic force field and are being pulled back to her. We are being activated, aligned to a new grid, and opening to a higher truth. This grid is a telecommunication system that generates wavelengths that use the universal language of light to transmit messages. Our DNA codes of remembrance are in a place of activation, and the electromagnetic alignment will unlock the memory for humanity. This has nothing to do with the intellect. What is taking place is a vibrational pulse. When we are in a place of connection, we will feel totally one with her, Mother Earth, with no separation, and we will feel the vibration of a system of wholeness and interconnectedness. This is who we are, and many are feeling the pain, the poison, and the disruption of Mother Earth inside themselves. They are crying because they feel the devaluation of Mother Earth in our structure of thought and lifestyle.

The beliefs and reality of our education, governments, religion, and science—all of these structures are in a time of evolution and being asked to expand to open up to a bigger picture. This is why it is important for new leaders to stand and speak about the new knowledge that has birthed in them, so people can walk through this time of expansion without fear. Because we have lived in, operated in, and created a world from the reality of not understanding the power of our heart, the place of connection of all there is, we have created this old story from thinking that is disconnected from the heart. No human thought or human structure of control can stop this process taking place, for it is a pulsation of evolution.

Over the last few decades, there has been a new awareness, and people are being pulled to look at the reality of spirit, God, love, and light. Many have left mainstream religions in search for deeper answers. God has shown many different faces within cultural beliefs, with the organised religions giving credibility to the gods and the religious beliefs. The journey to the new story takes us to a new realisation of the universe and links us back to Mother Earth, and this is all a part of the new story of spirit.

There is a mass pulling happening, and there are many people wanting to heal the pain in their heart. It is like a trend that has become popular. This stirring, this feeling, this pull is not from our intellect, it is from the activation aligning us to a pulsating frequency that is opening the human heart. The opening of the human heart is a part of the next stage of our evolution. The sacred geometry of Mother Earth cannot be entered from the conditioning of the human reality of today. The entry comes from the space of the human heart as it beats the rhythm of Mother Earth's heartbeat, connecting us to all there is.

Mother Earth has within her sacred places that open to other worlds, and we have forgotten all of this.

When you enter Mother Earth and align with her, she will speak to you, you will resonate with her, and you will hear her say:

You are the people without connection to your true origin, and you are locked into a world of illusions. You do not know me, and you do not know yourself. You are the people of love and light, and you have forgotten. You have entered a new cycle of life, the next stage in your evolution. The journey is not through your human thought: your human thought does not know me. Your human thought will be asked to stand still, to bow its head in reverence and respect for the natural process that is happening. The place of access is in your heart, and the human heart has many stories that have never been told, for the heart was silenced and commanded to serve human thought. Your thought is the place of information, education, and it speaks to you in words of beliefs and conditions. You have been told many things, and it is with your thought you establish a reality of who you are. Your thought has the control of who you are, and there is a part of you that does not fully understand the power of the human heart. This is the place of connection and creation, and you have not lived in a place of interconnectedness in all the history you know. Your way of living and operating came from the thought reality about who you think are. The human heart will tell you about the devaluation, domination, manipulation, and control that it has experienced. It will tell you about the children dying of starvation, about wars, the slavery, the violation and abuse generation after generation. There is a lot of pain in the human heart. There is intelligence, wisdom, and light that has not been a part of the manifestation of daily reality in all the history that you know.

Mother Earth will say we separated and we disconnected from the place of origin. We are the people of love and light, and we have separated from the divinity of ourselves. We separated from each other and disconnected. She will tell us we have lived separated from God, love, truth, and light, and we have always looked for God, love, truth, and light outside of ourselves. We created our religions and built our churches of worship, knowing that God was separate from us. The religions hold a place of authority and are makers of laws guiding humanity in different cultures and different countries to create different beliefs and rules of life.

New ways of life will come forward and bring great change to human existence. We will claim our heritage back from the natural order of balance that is taking place. The electromagnetic alignment and the activation will unlock our memories. The forgotten heritage is the expansion of a bigger picture to understand that our natural place of existence is the interconnection to all there is. We will take all the pain off the heart so it is free to breathe its truth, which is a vibration of love, and it is in all humans on this planet. This needs to be a part of the creation of a daily reality, and the vibration of love has the ability to create a new story for all humanity. It is our birth right to take this back and take off every lie and illusion that has been put on humanity and set love free.

Of the pioneers of today that have heard the call, some question, "What is my purpose?" Yes, your heart has asked to be heard, and you have committed to your journey to do this. Some have questioned if they have done anything. Many have worked very hard to release the stories of pain from the old way of living, and the pulsating frequency has pulled them as it pulsates to a new rhythm of life. Some of the pioneers believed that it was an intellectual decision to hear and walk the journey home, to take back their heritage as they moved through their own evolution and expansion. Yet many started to understand something bigger was happening. They learned the power of their thought and that they were responsible for what they created. They now understand the power of their heart by the activation of an electromagnetic force field of interconnectedness. You can have amazing information, you can have powerful words to say, yet if your heart is not fully open, you will express this information from a place of disconnection, for it is with the opening of the heart that the love and connection is able to create a new system of living.

Many great teachers have come forth in this time of evolution. Louise Hay, Marianne Williamson, Dr Wayne Dyer, Dr David Hawkins, Ester and Jerry Hicks, Eckhart Tolle, Dr David Suzuki, and there are too many to mention all of them. Also the great midwife of our time, Barbara Marx Hubbard, and all wise teachers and visionaries of our day are helping this shift in human consciousness take place. Many of the great teachers are a guiding inspiration for many. And there are ordinary men and women who heard the call to change, pioneers of today gently taking the hands of humanity to show them how to be grounded, be real, and feel their feet on the ground. The masses are not separate, and all of us have our heritage in us. We need to acknowledge that we all came from the old story and that some volunteered to hear the call first and live the new way. It was in their evolutionary process of expansion that the pioneers opened the doorway for the mass population to walk through, and we are living in this transition time now.

A Voice for Mother Earth

The doorway, our freedom,
the highest truth shall manifest
on Mother Earth:
the call to return.
It is important to understand
tremendous changes, the physical process.
Time release is happening right now.
You will anchor and achieve
The greater reality.
You will walk through the door
and remember.

3

A Voice for Mother Earth

Since my activation in 1989, I felt a strong communication with Mother Earth. When I was holidaying in Kings Canyon near Alice Springs, Australia, in 2000, I heard these words, and my heart could feel the connection inside me. The words were from a knowing, and they did not come from my intellect. She said:

Tell the people my voice was taken away, and a world with no knowledge of Me was created. When my voice was taken away, they also took humanity's voice too. You have no knowledge of your true selves. You are people without connection to your true origin, people locked into a world of illusions.

I am Mother Earth, and I cannot speak to the people through the governments, for I have no voice there.

I am Mother Earth, and I cannot speak to the people in science or religion, for I have no voice there.

I am Mother Earth, and I cannot speak to the people in the books of law and education, for I have no voice there.

I am Mother Earth, and I cannot be heard in your thoughts, for I have no voice there.

I am your mother. There is no honour in your world for me. You do not know me, for we are separated.

You can search outside yourself into the stars at night. You can journey further and further away to other planets. Ask me,

*for I have lived with you for a long, long time, and the answers
are within me. When you leave me, I remember. I remember the
times of love, I remember the times of peace, I remember the times
of invasion, I remember the times of chaos, I remember the times
of domination, devaluation, and manipulation, and I remember
all the changes. They are still here with me, the entire cycle of
human life.*

*I ask you to understand this. Humanity has entered a new
cycle of life, and this cycle will give a natural process of change.
I have witnessed many changes, and all of them are still in my
memory. Humanity is at a time where it has the ability to take
back your knowing, your knowledge, and your truth.*

*The order of control that was placed upon your heart has been
reversed; a natural process in humanity's evolution will reveal the
whole picture of human existence. Humanity has been prisoners
operating a reality very opposite to me, your mother. All will
understand this as you all walk through to your own remembrance.
All will learn as my rocks speak words that your ears cannot
hear. Your eyes will open, and you will begin to see me in ways
that do not exist within your eyes today.*

*The present systems of authority cannot enter; they are not
aligned with me. Deep inside of all of you, your own heartbeat
remembers the rhythm of the Earth's beat. I am telling you when
they cut the cord to the connection to me, an impostor started to
live in all of you.*

*Truths were placed on you that do not belong to you. In
your great books of creation, many have forgotten me. The great
books speak of different times and forces that walked upon me.
I remember all of it, for I have been living with you for a very
long time.*

*Your own reality placed the knowledge of creation into stories
to teach the children, generation upon generation. The cycles have
been going on for billions of years, the separation, the wars, the
slavery, the deceit and the lies, and the games all come from*

thoughts that do not belong to humanity. The human race has been under the control of a force that is not their truth.

I watched it all. Many times deep inside of my flame of source, I ached for all of you, for you are my children and were taken away from me. We became separated; you no longer remember me. You could not hear my voice; you built your history without knowing me. There is no knowledge within your evolutionary process. Your thoughts cannot think of me, for I am not in them.

I cry, I am your mother, I remember it all. I cannot breathe in your world.

You are all totally innocent.

My magnetic energy field has activated, and this will bring changes, a natural order of balance. Humanity will go on a journey home, and this is a global activation.

You will open up to creating new ways of life. Many will not believe and understand this, and this is fine. All is well. The impostor will leave, and your thoughts will be freed. A new code will birth. There is a Mission in place.

Many have heard my call, and they are pioneers to the change. They have entered my energy field, releasing the bonds of human conditioning.

Full alert is in place for service of love.

The doorway has been opened; courage and commitment will be needed to stand up with new ways of living. Your track history of human existence lives here with me. I remember it all.

Take my hand, and I will lead you home where there is deep inner peace. My love is all-embracing. Your illusions require healing, and suddenly all of this world that you are presently living in will not be real. An unshakable commitment to a higher truth will be your journey. Humanity has become hopelessly numb, creating the misuse of power, and steadily all of this will be unveiled and revealed. Surrendering will be in your daily lives.

I am not a word. Your words separate from me. Your thoughts do not know me. You are all beautiful beings of love walking

through the doorway, and you all will remember me. I live in you,
so you will remember yourself, for there is no true separation.

I felt a very strong connection to Mother Earth when this vibration communicated to me. I was overwhelmed. The ordinary woman in me could not understand that I had a knowing and I was being asked to be a voice for Mother Earth and to tell the people she did not have a voice in our world because of our separation. This part of my journey has taken a long time, and acceptance and surrender were essential. I have begun to understand the ancient ones and how the tribal people often felt the vibration of Mother Earth and how they could communicate with her and hear her wisdom. The communication is felt from the heartbeat connecting to a higher truth and aligning to all things. It is like being one with her. "I am you, you are me, and we are one" is the new way.

I was an ordinary woman who did not have any understanding or realization of Mother Earth's importance or magnificence. Family, fashion, and friends were my interests, and I had a great love of God and people. I remember speaking the words out loud when I felt this connection to Mother Earth, and I said, "I think you have the wrong person here! I think you're better off with my sister, Kathy, who has a great connection to Mother Earth, or with an Aboriginal elder. I don't feel a very strong connection to you. I have little respect for you. I don't see you or your magnificence at all."

She is calling to her children. The vibration is within our heartbeat, and it's the pulsating evolutionary process. Many will feel the pollution and the poison within their hearts as we begin to resonate with the consciousness of this magnificent planet. As she pulls us back to her and in the process of knowing her, we will remember the truth of ourselves.

Our total commitment is needed now because there is so much to achieve. A natural path to the process of becoming whole is being revealed, the misuse of power is steadily being unveiled, and global illusions are presenting themselves. We see this in our news daily where the greed, lies, and deception are being exposed in the systems of corporations and business. Old rules are dissolving, and it is like a chess game between light and dark.

Mother Earth is not a dead rock. She is alive, and within her centre are other worlds that are connected to the universe and beyond. The connection to understand this is within our heartbeat. We have the same centre within ourselves, and the magnetic force field brings together what is needed for life's evolution. This divinity of us is the connection's power place that we have forgotten, and it is a part of all things, all existence. It is created from a magnetic energy field that lives within us and is connected to Mother Earth, from her centre out to the centre of the galaxy and other universes. It is the power of the cycle of life, which operates as a circle spinning and spinning. It is magnetic and draws to it beyond thought, and it is the vibration of *OM*.

The magnetic force field has the vibration of crystal light, the depth of fire, the expansion of heat, and it rises to a place of infinity and pulls in the sea. Water is a life line to the magnetic force field, and it filters the energy grid beneath the surface of the oceans. This magnetic force field is not a thought; it is the flame of all that is.

Mother Earth is a continually pulsating energy force and has a protective field of consciousness around her vortexes, sacred sites, energy outlets, and dimensional gateways that are in many different locations on Mother Earth. The locations will be found in her rocks, mountains, oceans, forests, deserts, and in her land.

Mother Earth aligns to the energy grid, and this pulsating frequency communicates from a higher truth. This information is not from the word of human communication; it is from the language of light that operates from a frequency of higher order and is part of the world of different dimensions. In the activation of the magnetic force field, it will align with us, for we are a part of it. There is no scientific evidence available, yet it will come as new science comes to light with the natural process of evolution that is taking place. The information that is birthing now is coming from ordinary women and men that have heard the call of change and experienced the electromagnetic alignment. The alignment is often felt physically, mentally, and emotionally. The nervous system is being affected, and it is like being rewired to a different frequency in the physical body. The evidence of this happening can be expressed from the many pioneers that have experienced the symptoms of the assignment taking place, such as sleeplessness, heart palpitations, being over stimulated, feeling tired, experiencing emotional rollercoasters, and feelings of madness. These symptoms can be the result of many different health issues, and after they have had them checked out from a health professional and nothing can be found, their own awareness will explain it to them because they can feel something different happening to them.

Mother Earth is divinity and a continuation of all there is. She birthed from the radiance of a high energy of light, the magnetic energy field, and resonated to an almighty force of all that is. She birthed as a flame, and within that flame is the magnetic force field, the heat, the expansion, and the elements of creation. This is not a thought process; it is a vibrational frequency.

In the activation, we will align the magnetic force field to the centre of our being, and this will flow deeply within us. This will connect us to Mother Earth to generate the heat in our hands, for it comes from the centre of our being. Mother Earth is the sacredness of a church having great mysteries within her. Her crystals have a resonation of frequency that is the natural flow, and she has built pyramids and cathedrals within her corridors and chambers. Everything within her is perfection. The magnetic force field is gathering and pulling in the law of order and balance to itself.

Humanity is coming to an awareness about taking care of Mother Earth. There are projects in place to teach our children, and we talk about survival of the planet. We have looked at ways that we are polluting our environment through big industries and the daily life of consumerism. We are changing laws to protect the seas, and education systems have put into place teachings of resources and the depletion of energy. This is all a part of going forward, as there is a bigger picture at play. It is all about us going back to Mother Earth for our survival and to connect to who we are.

The magnetic force field within Mother Earth will bring to her what is needed, and she will cleanse her skin and birth a new story. The new story is about humanity connecting to a new grid, a pulsating frequency operating from a higher truth, which is love, and this will help us create a new world.

We need our connection to Mother Earth, and she will speak to us, wrap her arms around us, take our hand, and say:

> *I am your mother; I am your food and water. You stand upon me and look up into the sky and bow your head in reverence. By looking up, you see the father, and in doing so, you have forgotten your mother. This is the separation in you. Who I truly am was taken away from you, and in exchange you were given a deceptiveness of who you believe I am. When you stand on me, what you are feeling are your own thoughts of me, but I am not a thought. I am a vibration.*
>
> *I am your mother, and I cannot breathe in your thoughts. You have replaced your own breath with human appetite. Human thoughts have no knowledge or respect for me. I am your mother in great pain and deep sadness to the depth of all there is. You have no comprehension because of the separation, and you are totally innocent. You are beautiful, and you have absolutely no reality of what you are creating for yourself and each other.*
>
> *My tears are not for me, they are for you. The scream deep in my soul is not for me, it is for you. You don't understand who you are. My despair and my total anguish are for you, my children.*
>
> *I ache deeply in the heart of the eternal flame inside of me. You are my babies. You are beautiful children, and you cannot hear me speak to you. You were taken away from me, ripped from my arms. You were all sentenced to a life of separation. You were ripped away from me, you were told you were nothing.*

You were told a lie. There was nothing I could do. You were told I was nothing, we lost the connection.

I am brilliance, the flame of life, the connection to all there is. I am power beyond your imagination, the power of creation. I am the totality of love.

In your courts of law and in the sacredness of your religions, they put a figure of God so high in humanity's thoughts. They always told you to look up, to look outside of yourself for me. You were never told that you were already here with me.

You were taken on a journey of history further and further away from me, and under your structures and systems, the journey was given full rights, honour, and respect. You did not understand what happened to you. You were taken away from yourself and from your original being. You are who I am, a magnetic force field. I am your mother, the divinity of life. The cord was cut, and you were banished from my garden. God, the father, was often spoken about as being something outside of you. This was the game of separation.

The rhythm of your heartbeat is the rhythm of Mother Earth's heartbeat. The rhythm of the heartbeat is the connection of the force within you, the connection to each other.

These words are felt from a deep place inside of me that is aligned to the vibration of communicating with Mother Earth. I am you, you are me, and we are one. This is difficult to explain from the human reality. She was speaking, expressing, and communicating from a place of connection that I had to her.

Separation

During this period, old rules
are thrown away.
We are experiencing major revelations:
the meaning of life, looking at our history.
The entire human cycle requires understanding.
Violation is often in disguise,
realising issues, the misuse of power.
Our purpose and commitment:
honour your highest truth,
freedom for all.

4

Separation

Accepting an ancient civilisation before our recorded history, invasion, implants of thought, information passed on to us, programing, separation, and the reality of us not having our own will have been extremely overwhelming and at times too big for me to comprehend. This information is not from science; it is from a deep knowing that activated within me over twenty-five years ago. It has taken me many years to trust this knowing and information, for it often sounded like *Star Wars* to me. I now believe there is so much we as a race of people do not understand, and we are like infants of evolution. When the electromagnetic activation took place within me, I was totally overwhelmed with what I could see. I would tell my husband, Wally, that everything is a lie and that the whole reality that we live in is an illusion of existence. I could see this and feel this, and it felt like madness for me. I felt like I went to the time before the separation on Mother Earth and could see it being played out. Yet my physical body stayed in the present reality. It took all my strength and love for my family to keep my sanity, as this experience was a living nightmare. I am a very ordinary woman, and I love the simplicity of life.

I am a pioneer of this time and am being asked to stand in my truth, to have courage, strength, and commitment. I know that when we are true to ourselves, future generations are blessed. I know what I express in this chapter will be very unreal for mainstream reality, and that is fine. This activation taking place for humanity is not about what we believe from our reality of our history, and this chapter has been challenging for me to put together. I have reached a place inside myself where the most important thing for me now is being true to me.

Separation is about the way we have lived, disconnected from the divinity of self, each other, Mother Earth, and the universal existence. We have created our whole reality of human existence from this place of separation. This disconnection is a way of life, seeing ourselves with me here and you over there with a space in between. What I think and do will have no consequences on your life, and what you think and do is your business and will not touch me. We have very little information or awareness that there is no space between us. This is an illusion, for I am a part of you, and you are a part of me.

An ancient civilisation has the answers to our separation. We will remember the people before our recorded history who were of love and light in the activation. There was an invasion of the people of love and light, and they became under the control of an energy field of fear. This happened eons ago, and the invasion was from a galactic world that is not a part of our current reality. This is difficult to explain, as galactic worlds are not talked about in our schools and, are not part of our education system yet they exist and are a part of us. As we remember, we will know a band of control was placed over the heart. The heart is the power source connected to all things, linked to Mother Earth, each other, galactic worlds, and the divinity of self. The power source was covered up with an energy shield from an invasion of the people of love and light. They lost their true power, spirit, and higher self. They separated from physical reality and felt fear in this state of separation from divinity. The natural knowing, wisdom, knowledge, ancient writings, and the heat in the hands were lost. The band of control came under the cover of love, meaning it was in disguise. It was a force that was not a part of the people of love and light, and it invaded and violated, creating disconnection from truth, and the chambers of the heart became blocked. The people of love and light began to feel alienated from their own love; they began to feel the energies of hate and deceit. This all came from an impostor, a force of darkness that invaded and violated the people. They began to lose their power of the light and love and started to feel the darkness inside. The energy of domination, devaluation, and manipulation covered the people, and their eyes could only see from the place of fear and the state of separation.

The people looked outside themselves for love, as they were separated from the source of love. The true power of the people of love and light was gone, and they were under the control of a vibration of fear, looking outside themselves for love, God, beauty, progress, success, and freedom. This game of separation was put in place to make the people of love and light lose their power and be under the control of a force field that is not their truth. The force came from a universal command not of this world and from another reality of existence not visible or assessable by the mass population's human reality of today. The people of love and light experienced decoding and programming. An order of authority had been placed over the heart, the power source, and this order came from a force field outside the people of love and light. The true power of connection was lost, the vibration of love that connected the flow of life was gone, and the people became under the influence of a new vibration of fear. Now the people would be easily controlled from an outside energy field of manipulation, devaluation, and control. Thoughts that were not their own became implanted as truth of existence, and all this was part of a galactic invasion of that time. This is all beyond our daily reality of existence, yet in the activation, many will remember the truth.

We will remember that the heart became a servant to thought, and it was silenced and commanded to serve. The heart lost its power and was under the control of thought, and that was not its truth. We will remember that we are the people of love and light, and this is our original blueprint from eons ago, for there is no separation. This is about our lost heritage of humanity. We were all born on Mother Earth from this place of separation with our heart having no power. This order of control that was placed over the heart has now been removed, as it was on a time mechanism of our evolution, and it has been released in this natural activation taking place.

Our religions teach us stories about the separation of love and light. The Christian creation story is when Adam and Eve left paradise after eating the forbidden fruit. They separated from light, God, and lost the truth and were living the illusions of human reality, disconnected from the original blueprint. All of this information is in our DNA. We have believed that we operate from free will, but our will became the force of something outside f ourselves. Our choices were created from this place of separation, and we can only come from a place of free will if we are coming from the place of our origin essence, which is love. This love was taken away from us. It has had no place of power and daily manifestation in all our recorded history. Our truth is the vibration of love that operated from the codes of sacredness of all life. Knowing its interconnection with all things it is not a word or a feeling, for it is a part of all there is. It is intelligence, wisdom, and science. This love is light and pulsates to the same vibration as the heartbeat of Mother Earth. It connects us, and this is inside all of humanity, locked in our DNA codes that are awakening in the activation.

The love became a servant to the darkness when the heart was commanded to serve thought. We have often experienced life having two forces, with God versus evil, love versus hate, light versus darkness. Thought was given the position of power, the decision maker and the law maker. With the power source, the heart, in prison, the thought process was in a place of disconnection and had no purpose to hear the heartbeat, the vibration of love. The force outside of the people of love and light now had the power and control. The people of love and light were implanted with information from an impostor from a galactic world and were told that the light and love was outside of them. They had no power, and the light outside of them was the power. They were told many lies, and this created illusions of reality to live in. We have been living the reality of this separation from the beginning of our history. We have created human reality from this place of disconnection.

The "I Am," the incredible force and power of love, will birth once again on Mother Earth, and this will create a new story. The human race will remember, and they will expand into the consciousness of their truth, taking back their heritage and honouring the people of love and light. Love will shine and expand. The light and heat of this will radiate stronger and stronger as we release and dissolve every part of us that disempowered or crippled the light, the sun within us. This information is all a part of science and a part of the bigger picture.

This time is a natural process of our evolution and the releasing of the separation of self. A birth will take place, and our personality self will die and mourn old attachments and old dreams. These were a part of who we thought we were. Humanity is being asked to take the journey back to the light, to the centre of our being. All lies and illusions will surface within our being, as these lies are often connected to our worth and what we belief about ourselves. The denial of love will surface for us to heal, as this denial runs deep in the core of most families, playing out in daily living, in all relationships, personal, family, health, wealth, career, business, and purpose. The illusions will show themselves in our structures, as many of our law systems were created from the reality that divided and controlled humanity. Look back at the journey of the indigenous people, the judgment, the denial, and abuse, and it was all protected under the laws of our reality. Look back at the journey of women in our sociality. Laws and religious beliefs of the day often state a truth of realty for humanity to live by, yet if you look under the law, what you will see is manipulation, devaluation, and control. The financial systems often speak about equality and freedom, and the systems are set up for only a few to have so much, which is not for the highest good of the whole.

Humanity is going home, back to our true identity, the totality of love and light. This is on an evolutionary timeframe and has nothing to do with your personal choices. You can state you have no belief in any of this, and that is fine, as it will make no difference to the natural process taking place. The journey may be difficult because our thoughts and our beliefs will hold onto the divinity in a stranglehold.

Our thoughts will not want us to see who we truly are, as thought has had the control until now. Thought has created everything on Mother Earth, including Love and Light. The light, the love and the joy on Mother Earth are us. The darkness, the hate, and the pain on Mother Earth are also us. We separated from who we truly are.

The journey back to self is deep, and the war zone is inside the self. The love and the hate in us will do battle. The light and the darkness within us will fight. The pain and the joy will have a game of strangling each other. Thought has reached a time of destruction, and within our own thoughts is our separation. Thought has divided us into boxes, and the pain of this separation within itself has often put us against each other, blindly seeking the lost part of ourselves. It is the architect of the lies and deception that forms our realities and seduces us into believing it was love and light that commanded our reality. Many times, we were told from our religions what God wanted for us, and it was about being good, doing what we were told so that God would love us. Many of our beliefs about our lack of worth and not being good enough to have the life we want came from a reality that was taught to us. Big businesses often market our reality so we believe what they say about what is right for us to eat, think, and wear, and how to look. These are all illusions and lies for the control of the dollar.

The greatest battle to be waged in the completion of the old story, the journey back home, will be against the deception and the lies in our reality that have come from our own thoughts of love and light. The truth will rise in us as the separation is released. Thought will fight this activation within us.

The separation does not come from thought; it lives in thought and is controlled by thought. The separation came from the power source, the heart, being covered up and controlled, silenced and commanded to serve the impostor of thought. The releasing of the separation is not something that can be learnt, controlled, or demanded. It is on a time mechanism of your individual evolution, an activation of an electromagnetic force field that will release the separation.

As the separation is released and the journey back to the power source, the heart, begins, humans will experience the letting go of any thought about one's self or another that is of judgment, ridicule, or denial. To view another less than oneself is to live in a state of separation.

The knowledge, the healing, and the wisdom are here for the expansion of humanity's consciousness. For the pioneers, it is important to understand that we are here at this time for a higher purpose. The game of becoming higher or greater than someone else through awareness is the game of separation. What we know is within all humans, and our perception of becoming so enlightened, so high, and so powerful is an illusion. The lighter we become, the more service we will be asked to give to others. The journey that has called many pioneers at this time, this call is a pulsating pull. It beats to a rhythm, pulling in what is needed for the letting go of the separation. We are all part of the whole energy field, and we are in a time of change where information will not take you home to the place of enlightenment. Those who have the ability to open their hearts will come through these times more easily than anyone who stands high in their perception of knowledge and enlightenment. The separation is deep in us, and we cannot see it or feel it. We don't own it, and the journey of release is opening the human heart. It can be felt in the heartbeat, and some days you can feel your heart physically aching. Always seek medical advice and check on this, and if there is no medical reason for the hurt and ache in your heart, you will know it is a part of the separation of love leaving you. It will often be felt in the whole nervous system, as you are a human being experiencing an activation of electromagnetic force field. You can have physical, mental, and emotional effects from this.

As we look back in history, we can view the game of separation between the male and the female. This will give insight as to how the game of separation worked and how it controlled and manipulated us as a race of people. Thought became the authority and the rule maker, and this position was given to the male. The heart was condemned to be weak and not to be trusted. The heart became the servant, and this position was given to the female. Her body and soul belonged to her husband or father. She felt her femininity when she was being obedient, and her beauty was perceived from her total sacrifice to give to others. Reproduction was her reason for her sexuality, and she was living in a society that told her that her intellect was below her male counterpart. If she questioned any of this, she was made wrong and considered weak. Her feelings of good and bad kept her in her place; she was a human being without rights to her own being.

The old story for the males is not to trust the heart, as it is weak, and they were taught not to go near it. The separation of love created for the males to be used and abused also has them create war, greed, rape, and pillage. History tells many stories of the male strength with no connection to its own heartbeat. They were told not to go near their heart, as they needed to be strong and weren't supposed to feel or cry. Many men have held the space of great anger and disconnection, generation after generation, as they have not had the right to hear their own heartbeat in the game of separation. Many men have worked extremely hard providing for their families, century after century. As we look back in history, we are able to see this, and many men today still have patterns related to the devaluation of the heart that has run through their veins generation upon generation. Many were not able to give or feel their own love, as it was taken from them when the game of separation created the reality of heart with no power or importance.

Great courage will be needed for men to give themselves permission to touch their heart. Over the last few decades, this has been in a process of change. For example, fathers want to be a part of the birthing and parenting of their children, and men feel they have the right to cry and to express in the energy of love. Humiliation of the past is felt inside them, and many are saying sorry for the devaluation of women. Men were powerless, and as they were told not to go near their own heartbeat, they were separated from their true power source. All of this was a part of the story of separation for men. The male domination and devaluation is not the truth, as it was a game. All are innocent, and humanity is innocent, for the game of separation is not understood, and it can be very difficult for males to open to this next stage in evolution, for it is through the opening of the human heart. If you go to workshops or healing centres to heal the pain and let go of the old story, the room will be filled with women and only a few men. because deep inside them they remember the old way of not going near the heart. This does not mean men do not feel love, sadness, and/or emptiness. It is often not encouraged to express these feelings fully. They held the position of power, and this was the thought and intellect. It was the control and decision maker, and it had fact and logic to its credibility.

To the men who hear the call, you are loved and honoured. Your commitment and strength are a shining light for many men. As you heal yourself and go to the dark places of your own family lines, you heal and connect to humanity, and you open wounds of the past to set all men free. Always give thanks to the men who have walked before you with all their struggles and pain. Their commitment to create a better life for their families and countries came from great endurance, and we would not be here today without the ancestor's journey. The abuse calls out loud to you, crying deeply. The anger is felt, and the rage is touched. The heart speaks its truth and opens to new wisdom. New ways come forth, the peace is finely felt, accepted, and innocence is understood, and the game of separation loses its power.

The old story of separation for the female was a game set up so they had no power, and this is how the feminine played it out. The truth is that there was no power for either female or male because the power source had been separated from all of us. The female was given the position of holding the heart space, and this had no respect or intelligence attached to it. Women's lives have changed dramatically over the last two hundred years in many parts of the world, and this is a story on its own.

Women of the past were half the population, without any rights or ability to own their own life. Women of today need to connect and honour the process that has been before them, the courage and commitment of great women who fought the structures and the authorities of the time to give us the life we live today. Many of these great women have been totally unacknowledged. They came from all walks of life, and we need to acknowledge the oppression that has gone before us. Feminism was birthed and changed the laws and freed women to stand up and operate in positions of authority in our world. Women took their place in the game of thought, the intellect, the place of power, and decision making. This is still in a process of change for many women in the world, as the oppression for many women is still a part of human reality.

The feminine is not free on Mother Earth because love, light and truth, still lives in silence. In the separation, the heart lost the connection and could not hear the heartbeat of life, the sacredness and the divinity of the people. The heart has no voice or power and is unable to speak to us freely. She does not have expression in the structures that are in operation today. From taking the position of law maker, a place of importance and decision making, the power of the feminine is felt today. The intellect, the thought process, is still a part of disconnection and is separate. There is a new power to be felt and taken back. This will provide a new way of power for the human race, as this is the connection to the truth of the heartbeat and will free all women in all countries.

For the women who hear the call, your spirit is asking you to assist humanity in a natural process of evolution, an activation of memory, a transformation, and a birth of a new world. A commitment will be needed, and you will need strength from your female ancestry line. You are being asked to stand up to the reality of our time, the game of separation. There is no true honour or respect for the heart in the old story. There is no voice in the political arena for the heart to speak. There is no credibility in our science, health, and business for the heart's knowledge. There is no connection to the wisdom of Mother Earth. Women are still locked into the world of separation, living the lies and illusions. They are enslaved to human thought and beliefs about themselves.

A new woman is emerging, one who knows that her journey is not from a place of competition and disconnection. She is one who has sat silently to hear her own heart story, and when she listened to it, she heard her heart cry for the devaluation of women and children on Mother Earth. The extraordinary love of service given to the family—she heard it loudly as her heart spoke to her, reminding her of the self-sacrifice, the abuse, and denial of self that runs through the veins of many women. The echo was loud and felt and was passed on generation after generation, with no belief or respect or honour given to the feminine.

Holding the space of the heart was the role of the feminine in the old story. The women before us have handed us a flame of light, and it has come down the line of our ancestors. This is the journey of the old story and we are being asked to ignite and unite this light for all humanity. We have been playing a game of separation, and it is now completing.

This is how the game was played:

He had the authority, and he was Thought.
She was told to be silent, and she was Heart.
He was Thought, the manifestation of creation.
She, the Heart, was powerless in creation.
He was Thought, and the decision maker was respected.
She was banished, disgraced, shamed, and silenced, and she held
the energy of the Heart.
He had the authority and the wisdom, and he was Thought.
She was portrayed as evil, week, seductive, and evil; she could not
be trusted, and she was Heart.
He was seen as strong, with logic and knowledge, and he was
Thought.
She was seen as darkness and the demon, and she was Heart.
He was seen as God, and he was good, and he was Thought.
She was put into slavery, having no rights, and she held the
position of Heart.
He was given all control, and he held the position of Thought.
She was given no control and was powerless, and she was Heart.
He was the light, and he was Thought.

This is all at a time of completion. It is time we face each other, female and male, and see the game of separation, see the beauty and innocence in each other. We will live through a time when the game of separation is played out. Our true essence is oneness, wholeness, and connection. As the separation leaves us, our world will change, as will how we operate within it. What an amazing time to be living in a natural process of human evolution. All is natural, male and female becoming whole, thought and heart coming from the same breath of life. Nothing and no one is separate from another, as we are all one and connected to all things. This is a new way to live.

Opening the Human Heart

The source of all,
there is no limitation here.
You may rise above it all,
between spirit and matter.
Pause and remember
within a sea of
peaceful wholeness.
You may fly freely,
a natural order of
love.

5

Opening the Human Heart

Opening the human heart is the next stage in human evolution. In the activation, we will remember the connection to the heartbeat of Mother Earth; the pulsating frequency vibrates to the sacredness of life and the wholeness of humanity. This is a calling, a pulling inside, and it comes from a place deep inside us. Fear can present itself as the pull gets stronger, and there will be nowhere to hide, and there will be nowhere to run. Acceptance and surrender to this deep pull in us is the way to the centre of our being. She will rise in full power, and a new truth awaits its birth on our planet.

The opening of the heart is a natural process, and it is a part of the electromagnetic force field activation within the human race. This is a global activation. It is a physical, emotional, and mental experience, and it is a pulsating vibration within the human heartbeat. Many people will experience this pulling feeling, as it is inside of you and pulsates to a rhythm of life, taking you to places, people, and things that will expand your world. A natural flow of life takes place, and your whole nervous system can be affected as the heart opens. You will not be able to stay in the same reality of life that you have been in, as the pull will expose to you what is not a part of the new story. It is an alignment with a higher truth like the radio station being changed to a different station. Your energy frequency is changing, and this is not visible to the naked eye. Opening the heart is taking the cover and the shield that have been a part of human experience off the heart, and you will remember it was placed on the heart many eons ago.

Transformation back to the "I am" is an incredible journey that humanity is being asked to take. Opening the human heart is a new code of operation for humanity, and we will evolve under this new code. This is on a time mechanism of our evolution, and no present human structure can impose its reality on this natural process, as all is in its right place and time.

The human heart has stories that have not been told in our present human reality. The story is about ancient civilisations, the people of love and light separating from the light, disconnecting from the power source, the heart, and creating games of power. It is a story about thought having the position of law maker, respect, and holding the power place of manifestation within human reality. When you open the heart, you align with a higher truth and a different world of communication.

As we view our world, it is astonishing to see the changes throughout our history, such as the expansion in our structures, including health, science, technology, education, social media, etc. One part of us is in a place of great expansion, having the ability to create the architectural beauty and progress for humanity. With the expansion of our thinking and the journey of our intellect, many now understand the power of thoughts and the ability to create our reality with them. Yet there is a part of humanity that is in a place of depletion and is dying. It is the human heart, and we have lost connection to ourselves and each other. There are millions of children dying of starvation, and there is escalating poverty, crippling inner pain, stress in masses of people, expanding crime, and growing devaluation of human existence. The heart is in a lot of pain. The feeling of no stability is rising for the masses globally, and the very structures that have provided us with a sense of progress and stability are very wobbly. Fear has the opportunity to expand globally if we do not understand the bigger picture of what is happening on Mother Earth. The opening of the human heart is a massive concept to understand and accept, for it is energetically happening and cannot be measured. We often need facts and proof for us to understand life, yet the facts and proof are in the people that are experiencing the activation of the heartbeat and the pulsating pull.

Thought will sit in a place of power and will argue, thinking up new ideas. If you listen to thought, it will make you doubt what you feel and what you know. Your thoughts are trying to work it out and understand the breakdown of the very structures of our reality of life. Thought has no idea what it has done when it commanded the heart to serve it eons ago. Humanity's transformation is giving a voice back to the heart, and hearing the stories of our heart's journey is a calling, a pull and activation. We need to give the heart a place of respect and sacredness. The heart has had great courage, holding the space and place for the intention of thought. The heart was always powerless, having disconnected and separated from the connection of love. The heart is the access point to a new world and has the capacity to expose the truth to us. Humanity's heart beats to the same rhythm as Mother Earth's heartbeat, and its frequency of energy conducts the same molecules that connects all of life.

The heart will be naked, exposed, and feeling very vulnerable in the opening of the human heart. The pulsating vibration and the activation are connected in the heartbeat. The electromagnetic force field that resonates here, aligning to the new grid, is opening us to a higher truth. Mother Earth is in communication with us, telling us about the amazing time of change we are in, educating us about the heart's position of power and the heart being a place of entry to birth a new vibration. There is a new story to live and operate in humanity's reality. This is a vibration of love and operates from the energy of connectedness and oneness.

Opening the heart will be very challenging for many, and the heart is in the process of releasing everything that is not its truth. The heart will cry, and it will cry deeply, for it remembers the separation of love. All will be exposed, and the journey of human history will be spoken of. Many stories throughout our family lines have not been spoken of, and often the pain was numbed. When the heart speaks its truth, the stories will come forth for healing and to be acknowledged and released. We will remember the lost babies with respect and dignity, the miscarriages, the stillborns, and the abortions, as they all need a place in our hearts and family to put love back in its right order in the family's lineage. The orders of love were often depleted in our families, in our communities, and in our countries through the trauma of life and history.

Pain came to many through the birth of human existence, and all needs to be told. We will see the injustice; we will feel the decay, and our hearts will cry. The sadness will be deep, and it will come up with the breath. As depression and anxiety are a reality for many, our truth needs to be heard, as our heart is in pain. The abuse lies in silence in us, and it finds ways to expose itself through addictions and devaluation of life. Many are numb and fill themselves with human appetite of illusions of happiness, success, and love, which creates a life disconnected to the source. All will be exposed as the heart speaks her truth. The pain of the old way and the old story cannot come with us to create the new story. It cannot stay silent in the natural process of the heart opening, for the pulsating, electromagnetic energy force field will take you to places deep inside to let go of what is not love.

When the heart was silenced and commanded to serve thought, when the heart was covered up eons ago, love on this planet was under the order of sacrifice. The heart's truth has been sabotaged, and so it has become the energy of destruction. This energy is an impostor to love and speaks clearly and cleverly. The heart is often cold and has no interest in humanity. This cold, disconnected energy is found in places of position of status; it is in our homes and workplaces, in our families and relationships. Most people have no knowledge or understanding of the pain within their own hearts. The numbness is a direct result of the disconnection and lies of deception, the abuse and manipulation we have experienced. We have absolutely no idea of the poison and the energy in the heart that is pouring all over humanity. The pain and denial within us take us away from expansion. In the Western world, we have operated from a place of competition where there are only winners and losers; someone has to be right and someone has to be wrong. The control in our hearts orders this. When someone isn't what we want them to be, we are right, and they are wrong. This is accepted from a heart with no power. We are told and taught what success is, what beauty is, and we are told about being good and bad. We are programed to believe the reality that is handed down to us from parents, grandparents, and society.

There is a vibration in all of humanity, and this vibration is love. It cannot breathe or expand to its fullest capacity with pain in it, for the pain is from the separation of love. Within our DNA is a natural code of remembrance, and this is being activated, so our human heart is freeing itself.

Heart will take back its power fully. Love is a magnificent, beautiful, and awesome energy force, and it has not been free to operate on Mother Earth until now.

Love does not love another to give love to herself.

Love is already complete and full with itself.

Love does not love another for reasons of ownership, control, or manipulation.

Love is in full possession of itself.

Love only sees love, for it is the total energy of love.

We will birth love and the sacredness of creation on Mother Earth, and this will bring peace.

Females and males will no longer walk away from each other. They will stand and face each other to create a new story.

Heart and thought will work together, not in a place of separation where one part of us is in control of the other. Both will have respect and honour for each other and operate from a place of oneness.

God and goddess will come together as one, as thought has separated them.

Coloured and white people will stand and face each other. No more will we walk away from each other. Thought separated them, and they are from the same source.

Religion and science are one and the same. Human reality separated them, and they are from the same source.

Creation and evolution will not be viewed from a reality of opposition. They will work together.

All are one and complete in the order of universal law.

Our thoughts will align with a higher truth, and this is connected to the new grid.

Our thoughts will resonate with the vibration of love and the energy is of oneness.

Thought will serve the heart as the separation is released. Thought is very powerful and can manifest its reality. When the intention comes from the vibration of love, wholeness, and oneness, we will create a new story. As the heart opens and frees herself from the pain, from the lies and illusions of the old story, we will release thought from the conditions of the past. We will forgive and provide a space for thought to stand next to the heart, coming together as one to bring peace and well-being to our human race.

Heart Speaks:
"I Am Not a Thought"

Full activation,
We will now step forward, reveal ourselves,
entering upon the time of completion,
human reality's final battle.
Moving through the doorway,
releasing our old attachments,
illusions are crumbling.
Many people are choosing to make the transition.
We are hereby placed on full alert,
reclaiming love,
wisdom, and power.

6

Heart Speaks: "I Am Not a Thought"

Love is a vibrational force field that is the pure essence of a sacred life connection to all that is. It operates from a place of reverence, seeing beauty wherever it goes. It knows humanity is innocent, for it does not have the truth of its creation. It sees the division and the separation. Love feels the connection and the beauty, for love sees who you truly are. Love is not a thought and has never been a thought. It is not a game and never has been a game. It is a force field and a vibration, with its place of entry through the heartbeat. It has a language of its own, which is the language of light. It has wisdom of truth that it lives by. It creates peace, harmony, tranquillity, forgiveness, goodness, gratefulness, and grace. It sees all people as one, and it does not judge or divide it, just expands.

This vibration is in all humanity, as it is the essence of who we are. It is not a word, and we have put words to it to understand it. Our words come from our thoughts; they come from the thinking process, for the thinking creates the feeling. Love is not a thought, and our thoughts are so limited to the greatness, the magnificence, and the magnitude of love. Our words cannot express its true power or ability, for it is beyond the thinking of our human reality. Yet it is the thinking that has made up the game of love, how to love, how to be loved, if you are good enough to be loved, and what you look like can help you be loved. There have been many great novels about romance, and we have made up rules around love, marriage, same sex partnerships, age, and different levels of love. We are now living in a time where we will understand the dynamics of love, the power of it, and this natural part of us.

It is the greatest force field in human existence. It has the power and wisdom to create a new story for humanity, and we have reached a stage in our evolution where we have the ability to acknowledge this truth in us. It is this love force that has the ability to heal everything that is not it, so it can heal the deception, the lies and illusions, the separation that we have lived with, and the trauma that has been passed on to us through generations of separation of love. Our own reality of ourselves, our worth, our self-esteem, our beliefs about what is right and wrong, they have come to us from the reality of others and what we were told about ourselves. Love will tell you that you are beautiful and you are love. You do not need to go searching for love to have it, and someone else cannot give it to you, as you are already it. To only feel love when someone tells you that you are loved is to live in an illusion of reality, as it's not real. Love does not live outside you and is not something you can control or master. Love is you.

We have been told many lies about love, and the pain from this deception runs deep in many. This game never looked at what culture or country it deceived, and it is a game that we have played globally. Thought provided us with rules, laws, and set up structures of beliefs, and these beliefs still hold the reality of love in place, creating an illusion of love and not understanding that we are love. When we meet someone whom we feel attracted to, many aspects of us are playing out here. Invisible energy plays itself out, and we bring to us what we believe about ourselves. Often relationships are based on "I am what you are not" and "you are what I am not." This was a part of the romantic way of making up the whole of a person, and it is often spoken of, written about, and songs are sung about "you make me whole" and "taking two people to be whole." This love is the old story and the old way of separation. You are whole and complete just as you are, and this is what true love would tell you.

When we hold our babies, we are holding pure love. We often feel it from them, but the journey of life starts to tell the children who they are and what they are not. It tells them if they are good or bad, if they are clever or dumb, and it puts conditions on the child to receive love. Often the parent has pain running inside of them, and even if the parent does not acknowledge this or speak about the pain, the child often takes the pain on out of loyalty. You can have a smile on your face even if your pain is there, and the child will feel the pain because it is energy. It is not words, and the child will feel the sadness. This is how pain runs through families generation after generation. Wars do not stop just when the guns stop shooting. The trauma runs through families generation after generation, creating decisions from the trauma. Unless the trauma is healed, unless love is asked to view the pain and see the truth, and unless the energy block of love can be released, humans will live with the past traumas of their ancestors all their life.

Separation of love creates itself in many forms, such as addictions, abuse, control, manipulation, etc. Love has the capability to stand next to the perpetrators and see with new eyes. It will speak in a language of truth and light, knowing all souls come from the vibration of love. Darkness can keep people company from the place of separation of love, and this is the only way darkness and deception can play out, by living separated from love. When a child is devalued in any way, the child feels the separation of love, and what starts to take place in the child is the pain. This pain has many faces and speaks words of devaluation to the child, and these words and feelings become the child's truth of reality of daily living. As this child grows up, this devaluation is still playing out, creating life for the person. The choices that are made about what this person has in their life often come from the deep belief that is running in this person. This belief creates a world of devaluation, yet the truth is this person is love. The person does not know this or understand it, for humanity has lived separated from love. This is the old way of our human existence, as life has created this person to live separated from love.

This is how we have lived in the old story, and many of our beliefs about ourselves are not our own. Many of the daily choices we make about our life come from who and what we believe about ourselves. Yet this belief came from outside of us. Then there is education and science, giving opportunities to many for a more productive life. We look back at past history, at our family, and we have often judged what we don't like and what we see. Many have let go of families because the pain was too deep and the memories too sad. So they live their life with no contact with their family, believing the pain of the past will go. Yet the pain is energy. It follows them and can show itself in many ways, such as our need for approval, our need to succeed, and our need to control. It can show up in our health, it can present itself in relationships, and it will play out in all our life.

This pain is often the voice inside you telling you all about yourself. You can leave your family, and for some people, this is a choice that is needed. Yet you cannot run away from the devaluation of love that was put on you, as that is impossible, for it is energy and is inside of you. It becomes you, and fear, confusion, anxiety, and obsessions are often the ways of life. At times, the pain gets covered up and numbed, creating depression, addictions, and a material appetite that there is never enough. We are told we have free will, yet our will is always from the reality of the past. Many of the choices we make in our daily life come from a voice inside us that was created from a separation of love.

We can feel we have the whole thing under control. We look okay, we try to be healthy, we have created abundance by working hard, we do the best we can in relationships, and we try to give our kids what we didn't have. We are nothing like the past generations, and we definitely are not like our parents. We are doing life differently. Then something will show up in our lives or our children's lives, and we can only hold the control for so long. Your health will speak to you, or relationships will yell at you, and the control and belief that you are fully in charge here will show up. There is more to you than you understand. There is a bigger picture, a natural process of evolution that will take you there.

Thoughts, the words we think, and the feelings we feel—what a journey throughout history our intellect has been on to finally reach this time of completion. We have within us the ability to ask our thinking to remain silent for a moment so we can hear a new voice of truth. This voice comes from aligning with a higher truth, and this knowledge and information is inside of us. It is available to us from a place of activation, and as the human heart opens, this expands the present human thinking.

Our thoughts have the control, as they create our feelings and manifest our reality. Many people have been learning about the power of our thoughts and how we have the ability to create exactly what we think. Sports and business people have ways of creating abundance and happiness in new ways. They have been explored from the reality of who we are and what we think, and if we think we are unable to achieve things, then that is exactly what we will create. The thinking reality of cultures and countries each have their individual journey of change throughout history. Viewing this change can be done from looking at the natural progress of change in our history books and the science that has played a large role in many countries when it comes to shifting the thinking and knowledge. Education for the masses has contributed to expose new information and knowledge, creating advanced technology in daily structures. It is a more productive life for many.

When looking at what is happening on Mother Earth at this time, it can be difficult to understand because the thought process, the intellect, is what we know, and this has created the world we live in. The power and intent of our thinking—what absolute power and change this has created for humanity. The next stage in evolution is not to make the thinking wrong or the intellect less than the heart; it is that this next stage is bigger than the thinking of humanity. This is why it is difficult to give facts and information about this next stage, because the intellect that has been the place of evolution and change up until now is being asked to stand still, bow its head in reverence for the heart to speak. This process cannot be stopped or controlled by our thoughts, for it is a part of an electromagnetic force field.

We as a race of people, the human race, have lived like we've had a blanket over us and all around us, with no way to get out of this cover or around it. We have been in this bubble of reality and truth, and it has been humanity's evolutionary journey. We have created our world, lived our lives not even knowing that we are living like we are. We are the only reality of existence not having access to remove this blanket or realise we live such a limited existence in the bubble of the planet Earth. We live on this planet but are not connected to it, having no realisation to the power and magnitude of Mother Earth. We have set up laws and structures with the reality that we have the control here, that we know more than she does, and we dictate what is progress for the human species without any true communication or connection with the home we live on. We have truths about life and death, love and light, religion and science, yet they are in opposition most of the time. They all have answers to the bigger picture, yet we live under the blanket that keeps us from the bigger picture, as we have no access to or belief in a galactic world. Therefore, we live as a race of people separated, divided, many times fighting and killing each other for survival. Some countries have so much wealth, and some have so little. Devaluation of human life beats a rhythm of life for so many.

The human heart is in prison and has not been free to express itself in all the history we have lived. The heart will say, "I am not a word. Your words silence me, laugh at me, and disempower me." The heart will say, "I am the vibration of love, the connection to the truth, and it is in the heartbeat." It has a rhythm of life of interconnection, for it is the vibration of love that has not been able to expand under the control of our thinking. All existence has been under the blanket of our human reality.

Love has never been able to be fully express, breathe, or expand itself on Mother Earth. We are now living in a time when the heart will open and release the pain from thought's reality of itself.

Heart is the intelligence of love; she is man, woman, and child. She is the sun, the heat, and the crystals. She is the sky, the water, and the wind. She is the rocks and the mountains. She is all of this and a part of the electromagnetic energy field.

Love's breath has no pain or disease in it. The pain and disease come from the breath of humanity in its state of division and separation. Our words, thoughts, and intellect declare that this is the rule and accept no responsibility for their actions. To put our thoughts into the breath of life, we separate from the love vibration frequency.

Through the activation, we can hear the call. This will not be demanded of us, and if we listen, we will feel the pull within our own heartbeat. We will resonate with this force field in all of life, and we will hear it in the birds. Many birds are finding it hard to breathe in our present vibration of operation. We will resonate with the trees, as the energy field is the same as ours. Many trees are being lost through deforestation. We can hear her, our Mother Earth, in the fish and the seas being poisoned, and we will hear her in the starving children. We are a part of all of this, yet our eyes do not see, our ears do not hear, our hearts do not feel, because thought has disconnected us, and we are numb.

Thought must own what has been done. It has divided, controlled, manipulated, disguised itself, and often spoke words of love, equality, and freedom. But it has always been a game of love, with love being outside of us, and we have to get love from someone else. We were never told we were love, and we were never told we were all interconnected. The pain in the heart has come from thought's reality of love, and it must go back to where it came from. The pain must release itself from the heart, as it does not belong to the heart and cannot come to be a part of the new story. The lies will surface in us as we move towards the new story. The natural pulsating pull will take us there, and we cannot keep hold of the old way of love.

We have believed we have been living in total truth, yet thought has the whole reality locked in itself. Within the heart, an impostor has lived, operating in authority, because the heart never had its true power, and its power source is love. Thought birthed love in shame, and this was passed on through many religions and cultural beliefs. The denial of the feminine, women without rights or power, is just like the heart having no real place of importance. The heart was what thought said that it was, just like women were what men told them in the game of separation. The denial of the feminine has a bigger truth in it. It keeps all humanity in a place of disconnection to their power source, with both men and women locked in a world of illusions.

The impostor enslaved us. Love does not divide us by our colour or knowledge. Not one part of love would do this; only thought would do this. We built belief systems that white men controlled coloured men, and women were inferior to men. These belief systems stood up in our courts of law in the name of love, light, and God. Yet this was not a part of love; it was a part of thought's idea of love.

Humanity's reality is locked into a state of powerlessness. Some look powerful, and others look like victims. This is a part of the game of separation. The women in history were never inferior, yet our reality birthed the feminine love in disgrace and played the game, creating all of this. We need to take our thoughts off each other, take our belief systems away from each other, and give each other back our true essence, which is love.

To become empowered, to live from a place of our aesthetic self, is not to take the power from thought, the present system of authority. This power has within it the ability to lie to us, and it has set us up for the games of power. Our true power cannot lay dormant any longer. She, our true power, has served all humanity very well. She has sacrificed beyond giving us what we want, creating the world that we want and the world we presently live in.

Within the human race is a love that we have forgotten. This is a power we have forgotten. The magnetic alignment will start to pull us back to our truth, and all will be exposed. When love speaks to us, we will connect to the vibration, and we will understand a new truth.

We have lived this history, and we have built structures and belief systems within this game of separation. We have stood in total truth to this game, and we are very strong around who we think we are. We have laws in our courts that speak with full authority of this existence that we presently live in, and we protect this truth with great power. Humanity has been living lies and illusions, and our total understanding of ourselves is based on the separation game, which is that love, light, and truth live outside of us, and it is something we learnt, controlled, or felt from someone else.

The courts of law state that many of our truths came from love and light, which often means it came from God, and this was the reasoning behind many of the rules around equality, respectability, and righteousness. People put their hand on the Bible before speaking in a court of law, meaning that they are speaking the truth, as they swear to God that they are saying the truth. God played a big part in the righteousness of a lot of our belief systems of what is right and wrong, good and bad, evil and holy. Many of our unjust decisions throughout history were made in our courts of law, which harmed, trod on, and devalued people. This was not God, and this was our illusion and reality of a God that was outside of us, that came from the religions with power.

The reality and laws around slavery were implemented from a belief of God and good. Indigenous people were thought of as being inferior to white people, and this belief was stamped with total approval by the courts of law that stated their intentions came from the highest good for all. As it came from a court of law and stood under an umbrella of a perception of God, it was believed as truth, and people took this on. This controlled people. But the laws really came from ignorance separated from God. Look back in history, and you will see this game played under the orders of what were the beliefs of equality and goodness.

Today there is still the memory of the old structure of beliefs, and it is still played out in many countries. The story of human rights needs to stand out as one of the highest agendas globally for the human race to bring equality for all people.

Love and light are a part of the magnetic force field, a vibration of life connected to all things, oneness and wholeness. We lost this part of us. Thought took what was a part of love and light and created an impostor of love and then set up the orders of authority, the religions, and the courts of laws to protect the impostor.

A program was put in place where we created love and light outside of us. Thought told us that the truth was from God, and as a result, we created a God that had many faces and many religions. The religions on our planet separated us, divided us, and controlled us. They all speak of a greater power, a God of worship that has many rules, and different beliefs about divinity, the connection to life and the right way of living. What holds the power of the religions is the strong belief of God's word, and this word of God has many different concepts of right and wrong. Culture and countries play a big part in the dynamics of beliefs. Life after death has contributed to different ways of understanding life throughout our history, and the word *love* is always connected to God. This love has had many conditions put on it, depending on where and what time in history we are born.

We all have lived this lie, and we created the world we live in from this perspective of ourselves. It was never our truth, yet all was created from a truth of the old way, the old story of humanity. This needs to have respect, honour, and gratitude given to it, for it has been our journey of evolving. Now we are at a time of completion. The game of love, light, and truth still stands strong today in many of the old stories. Many people still believe that God is something separate from us and that love comes to us when someone else loves us. Some do have the intellect and the ability to understand the new story that is being birthed. However, our thoughts may find it difficult to comprehend.

This next stage of our evolution is not a part of a thought process, so what we think about it, what we believe or don't believe, will have no consequences on the letting go of the old reality of love, light, and truth. There is a plan in place, and all is on time. Some people have gone first, as they heard the call of change and felt the pulsating pull. It was their time to be exposed to a bigger picture, and these pioneers of our day will help the masses to remember. Many people will want to hang on tightly to the old story, not wanting change and frightened of the outcome of change. It is is not a choice of whether we can accept this change; it is bigger. It is our birth right to see the truth, to go back to the essence inside of us that is the vibration of love and light. The timeframe for this cannot be from the timeframe of a thought process. It is from a time of human evolution.

Many people will ask for intellectual answers as to how they can evolve and see the truth, as we need this to make logical sense of what is happening and the consequences to our life. We want an order, steps to take, and the information in a box so that if we want to, we can take those steps to the new story. But this next stage cannot be put in a box or into steps or an order. It's an organic, co-creating, interconnection process, and our birth right. It comes from a pull that is deep inside of our hearts, and the pull gets stronger. It pulsates and vibrates to a natural rhythm of human evolution. It beats like a heartbeat within our own heartbeat.

It's something that you cannot ignore as the calling gets louder. It is something that you will find is hard to describe or explain to someone else because it has no rational explanation. However, if you meet someone that has the calling or the pull, instantly they will know what you are talking about. It's an electromagnetic force field and a place inside us that connects us to all things. Yet there is very little information in science available for us to comprehend this side of us. New science pioneers are giving us information on this now as we open up to it. It's not based on evidence, facts, or something you can touch, as it is a force field. All we can do is give our intellect information so we have an understanding of what's happening. The natural process of this is the opening of the heart. It's scientific, and it's the centre of change for humanity.

The feminine is in the time of expanding in all of us, and she is birthing the totality of who she is with humanity. She is beyond gender, and when the heart speaks, she will say the feminine is the essence of the totality of love. The masculine is the power and the strength of thought. Both are within us, not separated, and a part of the whole global brain, heart, and mind as one.

The journey of the intellect has taken us far in creating incredible technology, medicine, and great science. We have unlocked many of the limitations in our human mind, and the journey has been extraordinary.

As we look back in history and see what the heart has created as a result of not having its true power, we will see the pain, disease, war, hunger, devaluation, domination, manipulation, and control. We have not comprehended the impact on us or on the operation of daily life. When we commanded the heart to serve thought, the heart was poisoned, numbed, and separated from itself. It is dying. The energy from the heart is in denial of itself, as the heart's true power source is love. Thought's control over the heart is out of control, and it puts poison into the seas, mountains, rocks, and humanity. As thought is ruling the heart, it is in control and operates from separation. It is thought's reality to keep us under the blanket that is over humanity, and if the blanket gets taken off the human race, if the heart is set free, then the connection of interconnection to all there is will be exposed to us, and the control of human reality will lose its power. At this time, the heart's energy is the creation of destruction, darkness, and denial, creating mass pain, and it is under the protection of thought. We cannot manifest just from thought. It needs to come from the desire and energy field of creation.

Intention comes from thought, and it uses the creativity of the heart to manifest our desires. Our desires come from a place of disconnection, the old story and the old way. Thought does not know who we are, and without heart, it cannot manifest on its own. Thought has been in control on Mother Earth, and we are now at a time of completion, as the heart's calling is part of the next stage of our evolution.

Most of the behaviour of devaluation, domination, manipulation, and control is accepted as completely rational, logical, and of supreme intelligence. There is enough food on the planet to feed the entire population, yet it's just not a priority under the ethics and order of control that are in the positions of power. Poverty does not have to live here on Mother Earth, but the money game in power keeps the control of wealth distributed to a very few. Many people have so many beliefs and conditions that have been put on them about money. For example, money is greedy, money is bad, money harms people, and money controls people. It's these beliefs systems that keep the game in place and poverty growing. Money is just an exchange of energy and whatever we put on it. Centuries of cultural beliefs that have been put on the people through religions and power places have kept the money game in place.

Devaluation of women is still a global issue. It has been a long journey, and for many women, it has improved. It birthed from a place of logical and supreme intelligence and it has major consequences to women on Mother Earth. Some of our sisters are still being sold as sex slaves, and mutilation is still happening. Many women on the planet still live in this place of powerlessness, which creates turmoil for the children that are born from these women. To create global well-being for our children, first the women need to have their power and place of respect in all societies.

We are living the game and are in a place of illusion. Our governments protect the illusion, science supports it with fact, religions honour it, and we, the people, are the operators of the illusion of separation. We are the destruction, pain, poverty, starvation, and disease. We are not separate; I am you, you are me, and we are one.

The creative force and ability to create comes from the heart. The intent and visualisation of thought is still played out from the disconnection of the divinity of self. It is sometimes very difficult to let go of the old way because our belief system stands so strong in total integrity of our truth about ourselves and what we understand about life. We have gone to war and stood up in courts of law for the belief in the separation. For example, the Australian Aborigines and women could not vote in our systems of power up until a hundred years ago. Many of their personal rights, such as owning land and holding positions of education, have been a natural progression in the last hundred years. Many of the laws were forced to change.

Science, religions, and education often preached and taught this separation, not truly understanding that their reality was coming from a limited understanding of who the human race is. It is all we have known. Often, your own thought, your own intellect, will not accept this knowledge easily because many strongly believe in the logical understanding of the limiting belief of human existence. This belief will stand up and fight for what it knows. To have intention from the reality of thought is to come from the old story because thought does not know who we are. We never came from a thought; we were birthed from the electromagnet force field that is a part of all there is.

The heart is operating from appetite, and we have disfigured its energy and disempowered the truth. The heart has the power to bring humanity back home, as the heartbeat has the remembrance in it. The electromagnetic alignment access is in the heart, so it is the heart that will bring humanity through to open the new story.

Love is the greatest energy that resonates from the electromagnetic force field that is accessible to humanity. It is our natural essence, and it is here to be birthed. Many midwifes have been preparing for this birth. Birthing love is the shift of consciousness of the human reality that we are being asked to participate in. It is the transformation of letting go of the old story and entering the new story. Love will set itself free so it can breathe to its fullest capacity. And it will demand that thought will never touch it again.

In our conditioning and beliefs that came from thought, we were told what was love and light. As we move towards the new story, we will begin to see that what we saw as love and light was often denial, deceit, and lies. We will see this in our systems of religions, governments, business, etc. What we have lived as truth was not the truth; it is an illusion of the truth.

As the heart releases the pain, it will speak its truth. The heart will become stronger and will expand, showing us new ways. In the process of the heart freeing itself, we may yearn for old realities that we have loved and known of, as they are the truth by which we lived, believed, and understood life. However, this place of the old reality that we held high in the heart lied to us. This lie was not one of intent; this lie is humanity's evolutionary process. We are innocent, totally innocent.

Entering the new story is not about destruction of our old story; it is about unlocking doors that have been closed for the entirety of our known recorded history. The lost knowledge will release humanity from the sleep it has been in and will take the blanket off that has been over us. We will see that the darkness built our structures under the illusion of light. We have been seduced with words of equality, freedom, peace, God, and love. The darkness on Mother Earth has come from thought, and thought has locked its energy into the heart and used it for its own desires.

Many of our thoughts are not our own, as they have come from a world outside of us. Programming and conditioning have been the way of life for humanity in the old story. Unlocking the denial of the heart and taking back the power of creation for the expansion of love is the next stage of evolution. Down trodden, unbearable burdens, enduring patterns of illness, and despair are the result of separation between spirit and matter. Our being is doing battle with the voice of authority that controls us. The human being is in prison through the authority of human reality. It can be very difficult to see, for the authority that operates now has had the control of the reality of love and darkness on Mother Earth.

The Earth's entrapment is that we have believed that we are the only existence in the universal system continually creating the cycle of life and death, generation upon generation, and separated from the truth of ourselves. We operate in a state of depleted power, creating the invalidation and imprisonment of all of us. The devaluation of human existence is often the driving force in many of the old stories in our history. The wounds in our soul are being passed down through generations. There will be no more cover ups, as this is the completion of the old story. The darkness will be set free from the heart, and we will see the pain humanity created under the illusion of love and light.

All of this a natural process of our evolving to this present time we are living in.

The Game of Power

Realising and gaining our freedom,
human conditions, human viewing.
Our hearts have been called
to remember surrendering,
separated from the source,
home sick and alone.
Retracing our footprints back,
we will begin to see
and will begin to hear,
moving through embodiments
on Mother Earth.

7

The Game of Power

We separated from the power source, the place of interconnection, the place of communication from a higher truth, the place that connects to the galactic worlds and the extraordinary residence with nature, the mother of life. We entered the Earth's atmosphere separated from the divinity of ourselves. We were born into a race of people, the human race, who lived on a planet called Earth. History tells the most amazing stories from cave man to astronauts going into space and viewing the Earth as one race of people, the human race living on this one planet, Earth.

We were born into families of different countries and cultures and centuries of different ways of living our existence. Many looked up at the sky for a sign from God or something or someone that gave purpose for us being here. We had no memory of anything, and we came into this environment innocent. History speaks of the great teachers of truth and love that came, such as Jesus, Buddha, Krishna, etc. Great beings of light came forth to show us the way of love, and they held the vibration of love on this planet Earth.

There is no separation from creation, but the human reality separated from creation and made up the game of creation. We live disconnected from our true power source, the heart, so games of power have been put in place for the creation of the human race.

Light, love, darkness, and pain all came from the same source and are not something outside of us; they are not separate from us. We are the light, the love, the darkness, and the pain.

Unlocking the denial of the heart will take back the power of creation for the expansion of love. The pain inside of us is a violation of our being. It has been placed there through the separation from our original source of love. We are encoded with a reality that is an impostor to our truth. Because of the disconnection from love, the pain of our separation, the depletion of our soul, and the misuse of love, we have all played these games of disconnection, for they are what we learned as our truth.

We have the authority in human consciousness to operate the heart as an impostor. As a place of no power, our intellect tells us many stories about other people, our judgment about what is right and wrong, good and bad, and it will give us permission in full rights to suppress the truth of others. We do this in with logical reasoning under the beliefs of our conditioning and programing. These beliefs and truths were often handed down to us from the culture, the religion, and the society we were born into. How we preserve the goodness of life and the needs of others is often from the place of acceptance of our own life. It is difficult to see the truth and the connection we have with all people, for we live in the violation and the disconnection. Logical reason will stand up to give you good, basic reasons for your judgment of others, about how they look, how they live life, what they believe about God and good. Logic and intellect will give you many reasons for why you judge, and your position of power is felt from this place of what is true to you.

Throughout history and in our present structure of reality, slavery, child neglect, children starving, wars, pollution, and environmental issues, our logical reasoning gives us intellectual reasons why these issues are in place. This also tells us the way some of these issues can be solved. Often it is true madness, yet the intellect will speak words of freedom and equality. We fight wars to create peace, and we make decisions on the impact of the planet we live on with no connection to her. The decisions come from our intellectual reality of what is happening to the environment and not from a place of interconnectedness to all things. It's all a game of disconnection, and the heart has no power.

The pain in us is not us, yet it feels like us, and we believe it is us. It speaks to us in many ways, giving us a detailed story of who it is and how it lives in us. Some of it comes from family, passed down from parents, grandparents, and many generations back down our ancestor line. Also, in the way we play the game of life, we became the pain, and we became the story of the pain. We believe this is us, who we are, and we pass the pain on in daily life to others—in our relationships with ourselves, family, friends, the workplace, money, and health. The pain and who we think we are—they are making decisions daily. Some of the pain is covered up, and many have no awareness of the operation of the pain playing out in our life. Many hearts are numb to feel the pain that is there, as it is not a reality for them. The numbness in us is not ours, yet we become it.

Much of what we believe about ourselves, the shadow self and the ego self, has come to us through the violation and depletion of our beings, and all will require healing to enable us to let go and move to the new story. We need to understand that when the pain was put on us, our heart was made powerless, and we had no connection to all there is. We need to go back and begin to see how we have been operating in life as a race of people that is so separated from each other. We live life with the pain making decisions for us, and this pain judges others. This pain depletes us; it is dark, sick, and lives in us. It often controls us, creating health issues and a life of lack. This pain speaks to us, telling us who we are, and we believe we have free will. Yet understand that free will can only exist if love is what is speaking to us, for love is who we truly are.

The pain dictates to us what to be, do, and have, because we live in separation to our true essence. The pain often gets covered up, and we think we are doing okay in our daily life. Some of us look like we have it all together while others are in a state of feeling inadequate and powerless. We all play games of humanity's evolution because we have been born into disconnection, and the separation created our truth and reality of existence. We cannot move forward unless we understand that humanity has been living in a place of misuse of power. Our devaluation of ourselves has given us the power, logic, and ability to devalue others under the order of a sane action.

I'll take your power and make it mine is the game played out in many of our relationships: personal, family, workplace, and community. *Taking your love and making you wrong, I will feel bigger and make you feel smaller. You have no rights. I have all the rights.* This is the constitution of our daily living and is called the exchange of energy.

This game created our structures and dictates the lives we live. It is the energy of darkness; however, we have called it the energy of light. We have law, economic, education, social, religious, and health systems that respect this exchange of energy. The exchange is often created through our beliefs of success, progress, beauty, equality, and love, and it has a stamp of total respect and credibility placed on it. Our belief of what success is often comes from a world of obtaining belongings outside of ourselves.

I worked in the aged care industry taking care of the sick and the dying for many years, with the present system in place. This industry has little credibility, the wages for service are small, and the respect for this service is limited. Unless we begin to understand that the dignity of life is the greatest gift you can give to another and that this dignity will stand with equality to the industries of sport and business, we will live totally disconnected to truth, love, and light. We can pretend we operate from a reality of truth, love, and light, and we can live from the intellectual communication of progress and success. Yet if we do not understand that the dignity of life has to be given the same importance as the quest for wealth, we are playing a made-up game from the intellect that protects its assets and position.

This story and the old games of reality cannot come with us to the new story. The picture is bigger, and the heart is pulling to be free and have its power back. This is our next stage of evolution, and it could be a very interesting time to live through. Yet the old games of control and power will hold on as long as they can. Many of the pioneers will tell you that as the heart pulls to free itself from the games of control, manipulation, and devaluation, it is often great sadness and confusion that are felt because the old way, the old story, feels good. We must remember what we know and that the pulsating electromagnetic frequency from the heartbeat is getting stronger at this time.

We all work with this energy of separation, and it is covered up and disguised. We spend our lives taking someone else's power. This energy exchange is very powerful, and it will do anything to keep us in separation. The game of power is: *I have no power. I have separated from mine, so I will take yours and make it mine.* This game is to keep us all powerless. We have no concept of what we have or what we are doing to ourselves or to each other with this game of exchange. Our present conscious reality of the old story believes it is our birth right to exchange this energy on a daily basis and to feed our own power because we don't have any. We have separated from our powerhouse and don't know it, and we often believe we are exchanging this power in the name of love. We are living a lie. We have no power, so we take from each other. Our love has so many conditions, and so we control each other.

We have all been slaves of control and manipulation, for our power source was taken away from us. We have all been co-dependent of a reality of everything outside of us, and we all exchange energy in a state of separation. This way of living feels normal, as it is how we have lived throughout our history. We are born into this world innocent, ready to learn the ways of life from our culture, our country, and our community. We have no idea that we are the vibration of love that is connected to all things. We are taught and shown who we are from a race of people, the human race, that forgot their connection to their truth. We begin to learn that we are totally separated from each other, that we have different gods and religions depending upon where and what country and what time in history we were born. We have no idea we have the divinity inside of us. In the state of our true essence, having no true power, we often need the games of humanity's belief of success, progress, wealth, beauty, and love to feel power. Believing we are all disconnected and separated, we can view others in poverty and in starvation as something that has no real consequences to thy self. We often deplete another to get a hit of power, and this feeling makes us feel in control and in charge. We will make another feel small so we can feel big. We will feel we are right and they are wrong, we are more and they are less. This is all a game.

The game of suppression is very difficult for us to see and reveal, as it is covered in the illusion of human conditioning. The game is set up for us to believe we are something less than we are, and it is very difficult to reach our full potential. The game keeps us in our place that is beneath, underneath, and lower than the position of another's power. The game often comes to us speaking words of love and equality, and it is often exchanged through avenues of friendship, partnership, and employment under an attitude of positive exchange. However, the intent is the very opposite to the words that are spoken. The pain in us is often in control here, as it feels superior and it will do what it needs to do to make others feel less. When this exchange of energy is felt, you often feel depleted, and the game is to do this, to take your power and to keep you powerless. To yell at the exchange of energy will just keep it going; it will not defuse it. To see the truth will give you your power back.

This exchange of energy will not come with us to the new story. We need to know that humanity is living a game of power, for we are separated from our power source and the place of interconnection to all things. Love has a new story to tell, and it will say: *You are all powerful beings of love and light and have access to a higher truth in your next stage of your evolution.*

The game of invalidation is under the protection of human thought. Our present day thought has total acceptance under the rules and moral attitudes, creating pain and words that numb the heart. The invalidation may come from all walks of life, and it is often justified from the illusion of our human reality. Many people in positions of power defuse the power of others under the logical reality of our human thinking. The intent is to take the power of another. The thought is to reaffirm that the behaviour is of the highest intention. It is a game under the present human reality, a part of the old story protecting the person who is dominating another.

The misuse of power is the operation in place under the ethics of truth in our human conditioning and is protected in our institutional structures. We are the operators of this misuse of power, an exchange of energy, yet we do not have an understanding of the operation. The game of depletion is to keep us victims in prison and disconnected from our true power source. The games are set up to deplete us. As we look back in history, we see the misuse of power through the power structures of the day, and when we view the deceptions and the lies that have been a part of century after century, we see that all are a part of our changing history. Many times when the lies and deception to the masses were in place and happening in daily lives, people did not see the lies, as they were covered up with words of freedom, equality, and goodness. It is with time that history shows the deceptions.

In the programming of the games and the way we exchange our energy, we are playing someone else's game. They are not ours because our natural essence is love. The highest energy and integrity of God has absolutely no power of manipulation, yet it is possible in humanity's energy of exchange to play the game of separation. We strip any form of love and light from each other in our daily exchange of taking power from another through our judgment, exploitation, and domination. It is very difficult for love and light to breathe on Mother Earth, as the energy of wholeness has nowhere to resonate.

We believe we live in integrity and light, and we have maintained many belief systems that give this a place of righteousness. The financial systems come in many forms and are protected under the law of our courts. They create mass money for a few people and speak from the tongue of equality and progress. The welfare of humanity does not exist in the old story, as the welfare of a few is what exists. There are millions of people starving on Mother Earth, and many people are living in poverty while a few live in wealth and abundance.

Our systems do not operate in integrity. The structure and systems create separation in humanity upon Mother Earth. The systems are made from human law and a law that was created from humans in separation from themselves. The systems are upheld by our ignorance, and they operate undercover, creating poverty, war, and disease. Our intellect gives us full rights to our actions, believing our thought and accepting the logical reality of the economic structures on Mother Earth.

The energy of depletion that came from the separation of human reality is now at the time of completion. The thoughts that have kept the systems in place will lose their power, and we will see a process of deceit, greed, and denial surface. It will not be able to stay hidden or covered up. All the lies will stand up and fight each other, and we will see it in our governments, law systems, social systems, financial and health systems. The game of power and the exchange of depletion are over. Remember that what is happening here on Mother Earth is much bigger than the game and systems of operation. An activation is in place, and the codes of remembrance are awaking, linking us back to our mother. This activation is on a timetable of our evolution.

The old structures will break down, and the games of separation will be exposed. Social systems and environmental issues will demand solutions. We have traded ourselves for a game. We live on a merry-go-round of illusions, which many will find difficult to get off because we have become enslaved to the illusions. We are living in a time where the human being cannot run away from himself or herself. We will see the games and deceit in our systems, the lies will surface, and many of the systems as we know them will dissolve. We want to take with us what is working for the good of all. We can stand up and show the way of expansion.

The social system is breaking down, as is witnessed by our mushrooming crime rates. Our material master has replaced the value of the human being. What we have has become far more important than who we are. We live behind locked doors under the illusion of freedom, and the game has become our jailer. We accept the reality of having to lock up our homes, fearful of others breaking in and taking our possessions. This way of life has become normal for many. Businesses advertise safe ways to keep all of our things safe and in place. Many homes have double-lock shutters and bars over windows, which can make you feel like you're a prisoner in your own home, having no trust in your neighbourhood or people. Take a step back and look at what we are creating under the illusion of progress and freedom.

The intent of the game is to keep us powerless and to give us the belief that we are powerful, in control, and have free will. The game imbeds itself in all the systems, and it is in us. Globally, we need to understand the physical process of change as the old story and the old games leave us. We need to grasp the reality that we will all experience as the power game is exposed. The structures give us order, the order will leave, a crisis point will be reached, and new solutions will be demanded. This impact will change our entire world. New ways will birth to bring about a new story for humanity, and we will feel the impact in our daily lives. Through the order of control breaking down, we will experience more crime and devaluation of human life, as the fear will get stronger. We as a race of people need to break through the illusions and see the games in place. New ways will come through an expansion of our reality and an opening of the human heart, giving it a place to speak.

The power places on our planet, the big structures that control the life we live, the financial systems, political arenas, business sectors, laws, education, science and religious structures, the technology, and the daily exchange of energy in these structures are often of domination, devaluation, and manipulation that is covered up. It is the way we have done it. What is happening on Mother Earth is bigger than any power structure of our time. It is an activation of memory, an opening of the human heart, and a pulsating vibration of evolution. The old energy of power and control is being exposed, and many people are losing trust in our political, financial, business, and religious systems worldwide. The games of cover up of deceit, lies, and illusions are being naturally exposed. There is a new way being birthed, and it is a vibrational energy force field marked by the new science of evolution. The power structures will need to expand beyond their thinking of the way we have all lived. Yes, many will demand new ways, for the old ways will not bring solutions to the global issues we face today.

Often the exchange of energy is masked from our reality of love, beauty, success, progress, freedom, and equality. Love has been under the order of sacrifice, and this was the game in place. We have no knowledge or understanding of the greatest power force available to us. This game of love we have all played depletes the power of love through its romantic connection to another. Love is a much higher resonance than romance and has the ability to view life from a new lens. It knows the interconnection of all people, and its essence stands in honour for human existence. It does not put one above another, and it never stops, it just expands. When a relationship is at its time of end, it does not stop the love, for love is not a condition that we can demand to stop, for it is a force field. Love is not something that we can demand of and dictate to.

This is the game of love that has been the way of life for us. Love has been under the order of control, and we have used it outside of ourselves. When love is free to speak and breathe its truth freely, love will view life with dignity and respect. It never stops when you stop playing your game of love with another, and this is a new awareness for humanity to understand.

The game of beauty is about devaluation and occurs undercover. Our heart's energy is disfigured and experiences beauty from a reality set up in competition, which causes division. Beauty has often been described with the essence of the feminine, and this beauty sets up games. It exposes the human to the waste product of jealousy, deceit, and deception as it controls and manipulates the human desire and appetite. It controls the way women treat each other, the way men see women, and the way we view the elderly. Many do not see the beauty in the wisdom of our aged population and the beauty in the starving children of our world. Our eyes see what our thinking tells them to see.

There are very few places for beauty to expand on Mother Earth, as beauty has been replaced by the human beliefs. We have lost our connection to beauty, and we believe what is marketed to us is beauty. The game is domination, devaluation, and manipulation, and the intent is to take our power. The reality of the game of beauty at this time is darkness and is dressed up as love and light. Ugliness is not what our thoughts tell us; it is our thoughts that are ugly with their judgment, ridicule, and deception about each other. The exchange of energy under cover is very ugly and deceitful. It is a game, and it controls many of us.

We have not understood our disconnection from our true self, as we have had no true power or free will. We are told we have the ability to create great material wealth, and in obtaining our possessions, we feel our place of importance in the world, showing itself as respectability and success. Our place in society is dictated by our ability to obtain outside ourselves. We have become the game. In our hearts, there is now an appetite that cannot be satisfied, and it is all a game, a depletion of energy, and an illusion. Many have fallen in love with the lies and illusion, giving their lies a place of honour and respect. We believe what we have been told, and this is often difficult for us to understand, as we are innocent. In the new story, the veil will be lifted.

Some people find it very difficult to live with the games, the illusions, and the lies. Some look like they are victims of the games of power on Mother Earth, often living in a state of inner confusion, denial, and pain, and feeling like they cannot speak, as they have been silenced. They have become victims of the consciousness of the present authority, as the game is designed to keep us powerless through unjust circumstances. The game takes our power and depletes us. The pain is locked inside of us, creating long patterns of misery, addiction, denial, abuse, and making us the victims of the game within society. We are told many lies, and we believe them. The game of victim is a set up. The authority of power works undercover, giving itself logical reasons for its beliefs and behaviour. The positions of power are repulsed with the attitudes and beliefs of the society's victims. Judgment and superiority are exchanged in energy, and very little responsibility is accepted by the one in position of authority. This game is set up, and the people holding the position of power, the structures of power, are happy to keep this game in place. *I will take your power and make it mine. You are powerless and less than me.* In the new story, there is a new way to understand the love and beauty inside each of us. As the veil lifts in the new story, many will understand why they could never align with the lies and illusions of the old story, as many of their beliefs about themselves were not truth. Once the veil is lifted, it will help many remember and gain their power back.

The reality in the old story gives logical reasons to keep us where we are, giving others the authority to tell us who we are through the games of success, beauty, progress, love, etc. We are not what the games dictate, yet we are told many times that we are inadequate, stupid, ugly, untrustworthy, useless, and worthless. We are told many lies about ourselves, and the game is to keep us in a state of being less than what we are and powerless so that we never know the truth of the magnificence of ourselves.

It may be difficult for people who love the illusions and the games to let go of them. They will want to hold onto the old story and the old way as long as possible, for it is what is known and accepted and understood. It has given them a belief about themselves through success, progress, and worth. It may be very difficult for many people to hear their own heartbeat because it beats to the authority and control of the human conditioning of the old story.

If we put our hand on a rock, all we can feel and see is the physical condition of the rock. There is knowledge and wisdom in the rock, but we cannot access this with our present belief system. If we put our hand on a tree, all we see is the physical condition of the tree. There is a life force, a consciousness that exists within the tree, but we cannot access this within our present belief system. If we put our hand on another human being, all we see is the physical conditioning of the human being; we cannot see or feel the magnificence of the divinity of the person.

We are all victims, and some of us play games to be victims of society, having no empowerment to produce a life of abundance, happiness, and health. Then there are the victims of life who live the illusions having no conscious understanding that they are living in a state of imprisonment. All of us are powerless without the knowledge of who we are, and this is all at a time of completion, as we are taking back our heritage, our ownership of our truth, the people of love and light. We made up the old story of power games, our power was taken away from us, and we have operated throughout history in this state. To take back our power, we need to have information about the bigger picture of our human existence.

Know we are not what we have been told.

Realise the programming of games, lies, and illusion were set up.

Accept that we have been operating from the misuse of power, domination, devaluation, and manipulation.

Accept that somewhere deep inside of us, we have gone into an agreement to operate the misuse of power.

Take responsibility, heal the pain in our heart, and journey back to our true self.

For many, the information will have no meaning or purpose, as they are happy to stay in the old story of creation. Many will feel and experience change, and this change will be exposed in the very structures that we have lived with and that have provided us with stability and progress. We will remember that what is happening on Mother Earth is bigger than the structures of operation. It is a pulsation of frequency of evolution, and you cannot control it, manipulate it, or put it in a game of our human creation, for it comes from an electromagnetic force field that is a part of all of us. This is the creation of a new story for humanity.

The Structures Break Down

The misuse of power,
important to remember.
Entire civilisations will move through
the existing journey.
Slowly all will be revealed,
dissolving how we have known it.
We will experience
a massive physical shift,
letting go of all denial.
This is necessary
to make way
for the new story.

8

The Structures Break Down

There is a new level of remembrance for humanity. A doorway has opened for world peace, for the development of a higher mind, for realignment with the magnetic grid and anchoring the force field, for truth to live here for global transformation, and for a natural process of loosening the present reality. The structures are changing the human race's natural process of evolution. We will rise into our empowerment, birthing a new story, a new world. It is necessary for us to have the knowledge and vision of this journey, a full planetary activation, and a higher energy frequency between spirit and matter.

Governments worldwide will undergo a period of intense restructuring, and millions of people will encounter moving out of the present reality. Our evolution process will take us into new ways of thinking and seeing, and many will begin to understand the bigger picture of human existence. This will give us new choices within our government structures.

What is happening as the old story leaves our reality is that the old ways and the game of separation are at a time of completion. This will change everything and change how we are governed as a race of people. Ordinary men and women will demand new ways, as they will lose trust in the political systems. Many view the games in the political arena as childlike, not having respect or dignity for one another, and not serving the interest of the people. New ways will be expressed as new leaders will stand up. The people will start to ask for the interconnection of all of us and that the starving children on this planet be addressed. World peace is possible with an expansion of our reality and knowing that we are all a part of the whole and that devaluation and domination of people are not to be accepted. The people will ask for change in laws globally, and a pulsating of evolution will be at hand.

This is a major step for all of us, especially those who have taken on the responsibility of leadership. There are many ordinary men and women who have heard the call for new leaders, and these are people who will be instrumental in anchoring a higher truth to operate on Mother Earth. The secrets of ancient knowledge will make their presence felt, and the new leaders will form a higher order of truth to govern our world. The governments of the old story will hang on tightly to their power, for it is what they know. We as a race of people have reached a crossroad in the order of balance, and it is on time and perfectly aligned with our evolution. With the crisis of the energy, environment, and social issues, a new way will be birthed.

We will create new ways, as the old ways will not have solutions to provide a place of stability for the masses. This will be a time of confusion, frustration, and fear for many because the old structures of our governments do not have the information within them about this natural process of evolution. Our governments will not have the answers for the global issues of today without expanding. They will need to look at life differently and come to understand the interconnection of us all as a bigger picture of who we are.

The games of power and greed in the political arena will be naturally exposed and cannot come through to the new story. In the birth of the new story and the new humanity, the magnetic alignment will unlock the memory for humanity, so governments or lawmakers will need to be aligned with the new frequency in order to provide a world of stability and wholeness for humanity.

The power source of control, whether it is with our governments, the business world, the media, or religions, will not be able to control this natural process that is happening, as it does not come from a place within the structures. The pioneers of today have the knowledge and awareness of the changes taking place. This is not a scientific fact or something you can see. At this time, the mass population has no interest in the changes. The natural evolutionary process, the magnetic alignment that is taking place, is not understood and many times not believed. The natural process of balance and the magnetic alignment cannot be manipulated or controlled. We will live through a change as we let go of the old ways and the old story and enter the new story. Many will have fear and confusion in their daily life and have no access to information or beliefs about the natural changes taking place. We will need to have the courage to view what is happening in our own countries and communities. Big change is already happening, and we need to remember that this is not negotiable.

This next step in our evolution does not come from a place of our choosing for the human race to expand or stay the same. The picture is bigger, and we are on a time mechanism of our evolution. This is not the timeframe of our daily clock or human thought belief. Control and manipulation have been in charge, and our human heart has called to be set free. This information is needed to help humanity live through this transition time, the old story leaving and the new story birthing. It will take courage and commitment from pioneers of this time to stand in what they know.

Until we understand our own existence and our own truth, we are under threat as a human race because we operate from a reality of misuse of power. This abuse is often protected within the structure of the governments and legal systems under the logic of human progress. In the old story, the present reality has no idea who Mother Earth is. Science and religion have no access to her. Science can split the atom, yet science cannot touch the magnificence of the divine spark. It is protected, and we cannot align with it from the information of science laboratories. The divine spark cannot be penetrated or separated, and it will not be accessed by man to rule and control.

The divine spark's protection is a natural force, and there is absolutely no entry to it except through the expansion of consciousness through the heart. Major obstacles, such as climate change, human right issues, feeding the population, the rise of instability, and depression, will command a change in lifestyles. We will not correct the abuse of the environment unless we understand the bigger picture of ourselves. Unless we begin to understand our own separation and disconnection from Mother Earth, we cannot enter the sacred geometry of our Mother Earth from the old story's knowledge and behaviour. We cannot manifest progress in this world of confusion, and our daily lifestyles will be in a progress of forced change. We will be forced to see who Mother Earth is. Humanity's control will not dominate the great forces of life within Mother Earth. The authority of human reality will be forced to take responsibility for what it has done to her, and people will live through the lies and illusion of human progress. She, our mother, has activated within her magnetic grid line a bringing of order and balance within a natural process of evolution. It is difficult to see, as it is like a game of chess between dark and light. Many of the old ways, the old rules and the old illusions, will be forced to leave our world.

The energy of destruction that is currently in control and operating within the systems is often disguised and covered up under illusions of quality of life. All will be unveiled, and in dissolving this energy of destruction under the cover of progress, we will all live through the repercussions of this illusion and the letting go of the control of power and completion of the old story. We will experience and live through economic, social, legal, scientific, religious, health, educational, and environmental structural changes over the next few decades. The game of separation is completing, and this will provide mass change in our world. The magnitude of these changes needs to be understood and accepted.

This time is not about doom and gloom and destruction; it is about expansion and birth. We are now living through a time of mass change, and the way we have operated within human reality will be exposed. The lies and cover ups cannot stay covered up as the new frequency is birthed and the old ways reveal themselves. This is energy, frequency, and vibration; this is not a word. This is the expansion of our reality that is now available to us, as it is our birth right to live and align with the new frequency. Our eyes will see a new truth, and we will see the games of domination, devaluation, and manipulation. We will feel it inside of us and see it in all our old structures. The order of truth is our natural evolutionary process.

The misuse of power will show itself globally, and the present illusions and lies will not come to us with the new story. Without the information of the alignment of the full planetary activation, fear and loss could be a daily experience for many. As a race of people, we will be asked to take responsibility for our actions. People in high places will not stay there if they have no awareness of the magnitude of change that is now in process. In the old story, the present reality loses its hold, and it is vital that we understand that what is leaving us is not our truth. Some of the realities that will leave will be what we all have known and loved, for we have no knowledge of the separation that created our beliefs and conditions. We are innocent. The energy of darkness was often in control on Mother Earth, covered up and disguised, speaking words of freedom, equality, and productivity.

The reversal is now in place. Some speak of a pole shift, a time of catastrophic change, a time of destruction. This pole shift is the massive shift of reality from thought having authority over the heart. This shift of reality is massive yet not destructive; it is expansive. We have been under the control of an energy field that was not our own, and this is a massive reality to come to terms with, as it changes everything.

There was and still is talk in the spiritual circles of some people that are not going to make it or survive the transition to the new story. They believe that only those who have expanded their reality and have something special about them will make it. However, the timeframe of transition is a natural process and will take care of itself in a natural order. The life and death process of human existence will still take place, and the knowledge of the death process will expand. But there is no group of a special few who will be saved, leaving the rest of humanity. Humanity is innocent.

The order of balance will release the control of our present thinking that has authority, and it will take us on a journey back to our original being. This will happen in a timeframe through human change, and we will remember who we are. We will operate as a species from the divinity of which we are, birthing a new code. The time of destruction will not manifest itself as some have predicted. As a human race, we have committed ourselves to go through the process of going back to our source. Our natural process of evolution is in place, and this is not a decision from our intellectual thinking. Mother Earth's electromagnetic force field is taking us back home.

We have chosen to remember, we have chosen to transform, and we have chosen to birth the new code to operate on Mother Earth. We have chosen this through our own evolutionary timetable, and this choice has not been from the intellect. It has come from a place inside of us. Before we were born, ordinary men, women, and children agreed and volunteered to birth this new story. As the old story leaves, some might feel as if their lives are turned upside down, yet it is the releasing of the old way that will birth the new.

We are living in a time when our world will feel out of control as we let go of many of the old ways and expand into the new ways. Confusion and fear have the opportunity to take the lead if we do not understand what is happening at this time on Mother Earth. So much of how we have understood life and how we have experienced life is in the process of change.

The present financial systems will dissolve, as they have not been about the whole of humanity. They have existed for only a few, and this is a part of the separation of our existence and the energy that has operated our world. New beliefs and systems will be put into operation under a new code of ethics.

The health systems will expand and will enter the new story from a place of taking back the lost knowledge, the lost wisdom, heat in the hands, and the energy field that connects us all.

The education systems will begin to expand and know there are libraries of great knowledge and wisdom within our children and the people of love and light. We will learn to tap into all of it because we are not separated from anything on the planet. This information is a part of the expansion and is available when entering the new codes of communication of light.

The law systems will create a new code of ethics for the divinity of all life, and we will progress to reveal the truth of humanity's reality in our daily life. The new law systems will come from a reality of interconnection, respect, and value for individuals and dignity of all life.

Religions will expand, and they will be asked to give the power back to the people. They will go inward not outward and know that God is within all of us and we are love.

Science will open new doors, bring facts to the expansion of human consciousness. Dr David Hawkins, director of the Institute for Advanced Theoretical and Spiritual Research, calibrated humanity to be at two hundred or less and unconditional love to be at five hundred. Most of humanity is vibrating at an energy frequency below two hundred. Everything is energy and vibration, so we can only align with what we are operating from, as the pulsation of the electromagnetic force field within us activates the vibration within us so we can expand and vibrate at an energy frequency higher than the energy frequency of the old story. We will align with a higher order of truth, and the old truth cannot stay with us as the alignment with the new frequency takes place. First comes vibration, then image, and then words are formed into our native tongue.

The misuse of power will be totally exposed. As we see the loosening of the authority of the present control systems in our society, we will see the massive force of greed and domination rise up to great power. It will explode, experiencing a process of strangulation, and we will live through this with fear and confusion if we don't understand that this is a natural process of dissolving and decoding. In the battle of light and darkness, our intellect needs to understand that we can live through this time in gratitude and ease and create amazing, positive lives full of purpose and abundance.

It may appear very ugly as the darkness and the games are uncovered and exposed. We will view the systems breaking down, crime increasing, devaluation of life expanding, social injustice, growing depression, and anxiety expanding. The poison and pollution will intensify as the truth begins to be revealed. Environmental progress will be challenged through daily exposure around natural environmental disasters worldwide.

Humanity will walk through what it has created. Humanity will walk through its own thoughts and beliefs and its own creation of separation, as we have been the operators of it. In the breakdown of the structures, know it is about letting go of what was created from the energy of the game of separation. What is not the true, original blueprint of us cannot come with us in this time of completion of the old ways. Living our lives with our family could bring its challenges. The ancestors of our past had many challenges as they walked forward to this time of completion. Always remember you have the strength and courage of your lineage behind you. All of us have come here at this time to be a part of the completion of the old story and the birth of the new story. A whole new reality of human existence is being anchored on Mother Earth. A new frequency of energy is being birthed, and this energy is a vibration of who we truly are, which is love.

The Bigger Picture

The doorway,
our freedom:
the highest truth shall manifest
on Mother Earth.
The call to return.
It is important to understand
tremendous changes, the physical process.
Time release is happening right now.
You will anchor and achieve
the greater reality.
You will pass through
and remember.

9

The Bigger Picture

There is a world inside of us that has never been touched. It is a world of which we have no comprehension. Its true realities and laws are opposite to the world we are now living in. The umbilical cord that was connected to the Mother Earth was cut and taken away from us. The feminine is not free until we connect back to our original self.

This new story is about a new world operating under a new code of existence. This code is within our DNA, and we have forgotten it. In the activation, we will remember the code we were imprinted with eons ago. This is natural and is our next stage of evolution. There are different energy forces from the galactic world helping humanity at this time and providing information to us through some of the pioneers of today who have the ability to align with a different frequency of communication. Under universal laws, the galactic world cannot interfere or take over. This shift is a physical, mental, emotional, and spiritual shift for the human race. We have within us all that is needed to take back our truth, which is the vibration of love. All is on a time mechanism. Our intellect is able to open up to understand the changes that are happening on a global level so we can go through this time with grace and gratitude.

We are not alone. However, we have lived as if we are the only species of universal existence. During this time, it will be uncovered that there is much more to the bigger picture in the galaxy of existence. There have been billions of dollars spent for the human race to understand life in the galactic world. The authority of human conditioning will only accept the facts of the present human reality, as they have no ability to comprehend the greatest computer of existence, which is the human being. Many people have contacted other species of existence only to be labelled with insanity, stupidity, and disbelief. We have the ability inside of us to connect to the universal mind and to the other galaxies. As the bigger picture is being revealed to us, we will be fighting within ourselves the centuries and centuries of old beliefs.

Inside the human being, there is a power that the instruments of technology cannot access. This power has the ability to access past, present, and future times in the now. This is not accepted and has no credibility in our human science today. The bigger picture will be revealed in the new story being created.

There will be change, and some will be overwhelmed with the changes. There will be upheaval as the old story is completed. We have the greatest opportunity known to humanity, as a natural order of balance is in place for this great expansion.

Thought is the intention of creation; however, it is not our master. The master within all of us is the "I am," the connection to all there is. It is more powerful than any thought that has occurred on Mother Earth. It is god and goddess, male and female, creation and evolution. It is beyond human comprehension. We are going back to the centre, to the core of our being, the centre of Mother Earth, and the connection to all there is. This is our heritage.

Love is the greatest power in universal existence. Love is the access point back to self, and love has the ability to heal anything that is not love. It has the ability to see through the illusions and the games. Love has no need to take another's power, as love is whole and complete inside itself. This love is not the love of romance; this love is the natural state of the being without anything else placed on it. Often love's energy is very opposite to the energy and beliefs that are held high by humanity. Love is sacredness, honour, and respect. Love's code is of the divinity of all life.

Throughout our history, God has had many different faces and has been used to dominate, devalue, and manipulate human life. Often, enforced laws of superiority and inferiority were put in place to control millions of human beings. God's hands were never instruments in any of this. The belief in God and, depending on what country and culture we were born into, the understanding of a God that lived outside of us, these became the laws because of the separation of our own being. Within the divinity of self, we will find the divinity of God. The darkness will be exposed in the transition time of change, and the light will expand as the heart is set free.

Looking at life in a new way, we will look at disease and health and will understand that our own separation has created the disease (disease), which came from the devaluation of the divinity of life within self. Health is the well-being within self. Disease is the denial within self. The health systems will be asked to expand as the bigger picture is revealed, and the lost knowledge that has been made available to the pioneers of this time will provide an understanding that we are more than the medical journals have said. Our own denial of our separation has created massive pain. This pain, unless healed and understood, will create disease. Decay inside self is a part of human existence and has come from the illusions and lies of how we see ourselves.

The great computer of life lives inside every human being, and we have no true understanding of the capabilities of this computer. It houses our conscious, subconscious, and super-conscious minds, and they all operate in the physical world. There is a new step to take, and we need to link within the mind to the divinity of origin, which is our highest truth, love. The way to the divinity is the link back to our Mother Earth. Breathe in deeply a golden ray and fill your being with a shimmering light, and the new frequency will be maintained.

A natural intervention, the activation, is in place to help raise our consciousness. The sacred places and ancient temples around Mother Earth are in activation, and many of the pioneers are linking up with these experiences and knowledge. The activation is connecting us to worlds of a galactic reality. It is an electromagnetic alignment connection and a remembering of the blueprint of ourselves and the planet. This new grid is a telecommunication system that generates wavelengths that use the universal language of light to transmit messages. We are a part of this energy system, and the grid is a system of electromagnetic frequency. The energy system touches galactic worlds and enters the core of Mother Earth. Our human body, mind, and heart are a part of the engine of this life force. This grid was a part of an ancient civilisation, and it has not been a part of the operation of human life in our recorded history.

This grid existed for centuries in the ancient worlds and supported the higher dimensions' existence. The grid is the greatest spiritual accomplishment ever completed on the planet. It was damaged and depleted from a time of destruction eons ago, and this grid has been restored for this time of evolution on Mother Earth. The restoration of the grid has been done by beings of light that are from galactic worlds and some of our own pioneers that were able to enter the sacred geometry of Mother Earth. They have been working very hard, helping to restore the electromagnetic grid. This grid instantly connects us to a higher truth of consciousness, which is scientific and is yet beyond the science of today.

How amazing are our ancestors to bring us to this place, century after century, holding the light and passing it on from generation to generation. The pain came through, yet the light could not be put out by the darkness of the pain. Love always stood next to the pain, holding its goodness, beauty, wholeness, and oneness. Many of us held the love in a place of wonder and beauty, often getting covered up in the pain. The light was always there. Often it was dim and out of reach. Conditions and beliefs disguised it, and there were times in our families that it felt like it had gone out. The pain of our separation from the divinity of ourselves was excruciating and showed up in all the games of power, control, manipulation, devaluation, and depletion. Humanity is innocent, for all we have created in the old story came from the place of disconnection without any knowledge of our separation. The old way, the old story, never allowed the light to go out, even under extraordinary conditions of darkness, wars, famines, slavery, centuries of hardship and sacrifice. When we are able to see the journey that humanity has taken to reach this time of completion, we will understand that the journey of evolution is not to be taken from the timeframe of man. It is to be taken from the force field of life. Change is a part of life. It is like our breath and is always there creating life for us. This grid enables life to exist in a higher form on our planet.

The timeframe of the completion of the old story and the birth of the new is not from our timeframe of conditioning. There is lost knowledge and there are writings that have been accessed from some of the pioneers to help us understand this time we are living in. There have been predictions and prophecy of this time we are living in from people who have walked Mother Earth eons ago. Many of the tribal people and the old wise ones connected to Mother Earth know about this time of completion and birth the sacred knowledge that runs deep through the echo of time.

- The grid is protected, and its vibration is love. There is sacredness of life, and it is only this vibration that can enter this energy field.
- It is here to help transform humanity and link us back to our mother and help us remember who we are. Then we will be able to create a new story.
- In an understanding of the bigger picture, we will remember. We will remember and understand the misuse of power and the games of depletion that are played in our daily lives, undercover and protected by the logic of human thought.
- We will remember how darkness had control of humanity on Mother Earth. We have been operating from domination, devaluation, and manipulation.
- We will accept with a knowing, open to a higher truth that many of our thoughts have not been our own, that they have come from an impostor, a force outside of us.

- We will remember we are innocent and we had no knowledge or awareness of our separation of the divinity of ourselves, as our original blueprint was taken away from us.
- We will be exposed to knowledge, and we will realise this history is not the only history that has lived on Mother Earth.
- Our natural state is love, and it is our birth right to take this back.
- Planetary evolution containing electromagnetic alignment will unlock the memory for humanity.

This is why the next step in our evolution is not negotiable. It is not from a human thought decision to participate in the evolutionally process. All is in its right place and order. If we look at our world from the information we have, the understanding of our own existence from our science and religion, we could look to be in a very vulnerable place at this time of crossroads. We live in a state of so many limitations and needing evidence, always wanting facts and proof that our intellect can touch or hold or see. What happens to a race of people who do not have the information in their systems about the truth of themselves? It is a race of people who cannot accept new findings of reality from the pioneers without proof that they can touch and understand. The bigger picture is enormous, and we will never understand it from the present reality of the intellect of today. We need to accept that there is a bigger picture and then allow the natural processes of life to take us there, for this bigger picture will unfold for humanity naturally.

The completion of the old story will leave behind all the limitations that we have lived with our understanding of the galactic worlds. New information is available that is being birthed and anchored and is opening us to a universal connection. We will live as a part of the galactic world, for this is who we are, not separate, and not the only existence in life in the universe.

The activation of the electromagnetic force field will pull us back to this memory, and we will link back to Mother Earth. She has always had the entire history of the people that have walked on her, and this history goes back to eons ago. This memory has always been in her. We just separated from her, and we will align with the new grid and instantly open to a higher truth frequency.

The bigger picture is something very difficult to comprehend, to even believe, from the ordinary thinking of humanity today. This is all on time and perfect for our evolution. We can obtain the information so that our intellectual mind will feel it and understand it, yet the information cannot take us to the place of remembrance. We can take on scientific explanations of what is happening at the time in our evolution, but this is not the remembrance, as we can still live in the energy field of the old story, the energy of separation. So our minds can have the information, and our hearts can still have the pain and the disconnection. This is part of the journey, and what we will come to terms with is that we will need to surrender the intellect, our thinking, and let go of the control that we believe we have had.

The electromagnetic force field will be felt in silence for the masses. This is a heightened acceleration of energy frequency waves, and this direct alignment will release the order of authority that was placed over the human heart eons ago. This will liberate humanity globally, and you may feel the pulsating frequency and the knowing in your solar plexus. Some may experience physical, mental, and emotional changes. Some will feel numb. All is okay, and some will feel the pull to let go of the old pain, the old story inside of them. All of this in on time and in perfect alignment with our evolutional process.

Prophecy from the Mother

We are at a time of
expansion.
Knowledge will rise in us.
A total alignment,
activation.
We are on a time mechanism
of our own
evolution.
We will link back to
Mother Earth,
and we will communicate with her.

10

Prophecy from the Mother

I cannot provide you with scientific facts on how this all works. I am a very ordinary woman, wife, mum, and grandmother that is extremely happy to have this role in my life. I experienced a phenomenon that asked me to stand up with a knowing of information about this amazing time we live in. There is no logical and rational explanation in any of this information. It is a strong knowing, and I have fought this knowing for many years. My journey of acceptance has been about struggle and hiding this communication. My alignment with Mother Earth was an extraordinary experience, and it felt like she communicated a feeling of sacredness, reverence.

I have lived with you for a long time, and I remember the entire cycle of humanity, as all of it is still here with me. You have entered a new cycle of human existence, and this will bring great change. What I see in the future is a time of transition, and this will provide opportunities for expansion. Humanity has agreed to walk the journey back home, and many will not remember the agreement. What a blessing you have given yourself. All of you are innocent, for you are my children, and you were cut off from me. The old story was birthed and created in separation, and this time is now completing.

You are living in a time of change, a time of transition. This will bring about days when many will look at it as destruction, and what you have known as truth will be uncovered as lies and illusions. New science will bring facts about the electromagnetic alignment taking place as I, your mother, have activated the magnetic force field pulling you back to me. I am your mother, you are my children, and I want to wrap you up with my love. This transition has never happened before in your recorded history. The timeframe of the transition is not from manmade time, it is evolutionary timeframe.

There is a storm ahead, and having knowledge about this storm will help you be prepared for the time when separation is being let go of in all your systems, structures, and in all your thoughts. I, your mother, see a vision for a new world for humanity. Take my hand, and I, your mother, will take you home, as all is on time and in its right order of completion. Fear is leaving you, and it will show up with great strength if you do not understand what is happening here in the transition. The people of love and light will remember who they are, and all will be a natural part of the transition. As the old structures break down, new structures will be born, as pioneers of the day are anchoring many new ways now.

The children being born today come with great knowledge and awakened memory. They will not be closed down from the old ways, as new ways will be accepted. They have come here to help the transition with new ways of living.

Some of the days may feel dark for many because the larger population has no idea of the time we are living in. I, your mother, see each of you. I see your innocence, I see your beauty, and I have watched it all. My children, humanity, you have lived on me separated, divided, and disconnected. The battle is finally over, and the birthing of a new world is here.

The transformation period will bring about a whole new way of being, and the game of economics and finance will change. There is spiralling debt worldwide, and it is out of control. There is a storm ahead that will affect many people, and denial will play itself out. Humanity is heading towards a big crash, and it will stop the game. Economics, anger, and frustration are on the rise worldwide—this is a global problem. There will be poverty and confusion in lands of wealth, the lies and illusions will be exposed, the greed will show itself, and there will be no more cover-ups—the old game is over. The financial worlds will emerge, and new solutions will be birthed. Poverty worldwide will be addressed as the separation leaves you. The old game of economics will hang as long as it can. It will not leave without a fight, for it was a game that gave great power and authority, and it has had great control over humanity.

I tell you this, to prepare for the storm, take may hand, and we will walk through this storm together. Your structures of governments and law makers cannot stop this natural process of change, for it is bigger than the reality of your governments and law makers. This information is not about doom and gloom, this information is seeing the separation of economics on Mother Earth being released and a new and better world being birthed.

You, humanity, stand on me, your mother, and you have no connection to me. I am calling you, and many cannot hear the call. You are innocent, for you were taken away from me. I cannot breathe in your world any longer, as you have created a world that operates from laws opposite to my laws. Poisons and toxins are in my seas and rivers. Your political arena and your sciences have no access to me, for they do not know me, and they cannot enter me. I weep for you, as you are my babies, having no idea what you are creating for yourself and each other. In this time of transformation, transition from old story to new story, you will be exposed to great changes. Global warming and earth changes have had a great deal of discussion in the worlds of power and law makers of the people. With evolution versus humanity's daily life, change is a natural part of evolution, and humanity has reached a crossroad in the balance of life. Disruption is in process, and this will create geographical changes that are perfect and on time. Solutions cannot be reached from the reality of the old story, the old energy of separation.

Your books of education speak about taking care of me, and many are teaching the children to have respect for me, Mother Earth. You cannot have respect for me until you know the truth of who you are. It is not about taking care of me so I will keep alive; it is opposite to that. It is about coming back to me. My laws are in opposition to yours, we are disconnected, and you have no knowledge of the magnificence of me, the awesome power and life force within me that you cannot feel. You are numb to it, have no respect for it, and how can you when you are disconnected from it. Your business worlds, governments, and law makers make decisions without ever feeling the life force within me. All of this will change.

Humanity will walk through this change, and new ways will birth as the separation leaves you. Great sadness may be felt as the truth is exposed to you, a race of people without power-play games that deplete and separate each other. Yes, the storms ahead will be challenging and will provide new growth and expansion. Confusion and fear will have their place for many as humanity walks the journey home. Transformation will be the order of this time.

Twenty-five years ago when the visitation happened to me, some of the first few words I could feel being exposed to me were: "If you could see the devastation on your planet." Humanity is at a time of great change. At the time, my reality was family, friends, and fashion, and I went into total fear. I have three children, and I was very frightened, wondering what they would have to live through. Within me, I could feel the money system breaking down, feel disruptions on the earth. I felt this so strongly that I was overwhelmed and could not connect to life very well. It was a feeling of what was the point, everything was going to go. I spoke to my family a little about what I could see and feel, trying not to frighten them. I often spoke about these times with the women that were a part of the activation. We had fear, yet we also had laughter to keep us sane. We loved fashion, and so very often we would say, "Well if everything is going, we will go down in style with our lipstick on and our fashion!"

I could write about earth changes, weather changes, the money markets crashing, saying things like superannuation will be worth very little as the financial system is changing, our houses will lose their value. There was not a lot to look forward to. I remember walking around Adelaide in South Australia, looking at the people, aching for them, thinking to myself, *If only they knew what was ahead of them.* I would go to social events, and the people would be laughing. I felt overwhelmed with the knowledge that was being exposed to me, and I knew the year 2012 was a time of completion.

I had no idea that there were many prophecies and predictions about this time of change. I did not know there was a Mayan calendar that indicated humanity would go through this time of change. I was an ordinary woman, just happy in my life with my family and friends. In my own journey of transformation, information and books and people came to me and shared their knowledge. I began to understand that the knowledge in me was also in others. I did not share the prophecies with many people because, first of all, what if it was all lies? Secondly, I did not want to frighten anyone, and who was I to tell people about this stuff anyway?

It has never left me, and I watch with great interest as I see the money markets changing, as I hear the sciences now say global warming is real, and weather storms show up in places they have not been before. Mother Earth is rumbling, and she is being felt by many. I often felt burdened by this knowing. Some people call this knowing channelling, and some ask me what Anton, the being from the ancient temple that opened up a new world for me, is telling me as if he is still communicating to me. He visited me once, and that was it. I feel that he was a gatekeeper, and he gave me access to the knowledge of this ancient place that existed eons ago. I felt like he entrusted me with the keys, and I then became the gatekeeper for this sacred information that is here to expand the human understanding. I felt that he knew I would never abuse this information for myself and only use it for the good. It was a huge responsibility, and I did have days when I was not impressed with him! Yet I now understand that my knowledge has not come from him; it came from an alignment with a higher truth activated within me. Anton was a gatekeeper for this ancient temple, and he opened the doorway for me to walk through. Not a bad day's work for someone like me who was only interested in family, friends, and fashion!

The fear has gone, and the burden has lifted that I carried for many years. We will go through massive change. Many of our ancestors walked the road of great change that is different from this change, yet the human conditions of commitment, strength, and courage have walked with us for many generations. Yes, our structures will change, and this is not to be feared, it is to be understood.

Some of the prophecies speak about humanity needing to choose to evolve to this next stage in evolution. I believe we have already chosen this path, as ordinary people are experiencing extraordinary phenomena. This time is not about destruction, as we are already in destruction. This time is about expansion and the destruction leaving.

Walking through the Storm
with Grace and Gratitude

"Take my hand," Mother Earth speaks.

Changes are on a global level.

You are going back to the I Am.

The umbilical cord connecting to

humanity is returning.

You will walk through and remember.

Everything is of purpose

and

alignment.

11

Walking through the Storm with Grace and Gratitude

In times of change, struggle can be our natural survival mechanism. If we have information that provides us with a deeper understanding, that the winds of change are here for our highest good, walking through this time of transition can be experienced with grace and gratitude in our hearts. As things break down, you can feel gratitude for what has been and what is to come, and it will make the transition easier.

I am your mother, and I will take you back home. The activation will connect you to a new grid and open you to a higher truth that will link us back together. We have lived invisible to one another. My internal flame is flickering, expanding, pulling you back to me. You cannot see me through your eyes, as they can only see through your thoughts of me. Some of you have heard me call you; the call is getting stronger and it is deep within you. Walking through the storm can bring its challengers to you, for a new way is being birthed within you. A memory is being activated, and the old story will hang on for as long as it can. This can be a struggle, as the old energy of separation still lives in you not wanting to let go. This is big, too big for most of you to totally understand. You cannot see this activation, you cannot see the separation leaving, for these are not things, words, or structures. It cannot be contained or controlled or learnt. It is your birth right, and this is a frequency, a vibration, a new way.

There is a natural flow of life, and many have discounted it. Humanity has been walking through life operating from a field of energy that is opposite to me, your mother's natural flow to walk through the storm of transition and transformation. Connecting back to this natural flow of life will take us on a journey of gratitude and grace.

You have controlled life with your demands and desires. You have often just wanted more and more, so you have learnt about the power of your own thinking and that you create what you think. Many have used this to get more and demand control and dictate how they want it all to be. The intent has often come from the reality of the thought with the heart in prison and under the control of your thought. The intention is not connecting to the oneness, wholeness of life, because the passenger of life is in a state of separation.

As the separation leaves because it cannot live within the activation and vibration energy frequency, what you are demanding and intending from your thought reality may not manifest, for what is being birthed in you is a new way of living. The deep calling inside of you will change and shift to a new level of understanding life. What you have put out to create will come if it is in alignment with your purpose and your willingness to serve humanity. This is not a time about you getting more, becoming important, and having position of power and credibility. It is much bigger.

You are living in a time of expansion, and your own evolution process demands this. For the pioneers of today, the ones who have heard the call, you have walked a journey of discovery, transforming, and learning. You have healed much of the pain that has stopped you from moving forward. You have expanded the boundaries of the human reality. You have opened to the power of your thoughts, and you have created new businesses, bringing information of the ancient knowledge through, and opened the doorway for humanity to walk though. There is more, as most of this has been done from the state of separation that is still a part of your vibration. You are innocent. You often see the depletion and pain in others with superiority and judgment.

You are ambassadors of the light, and you have been handed this light from your parents. You have been given life from them, and it has been passed onto you. Yes, the pain and the struggle came too, yet you have been born here at this time to evolve so that you will move into a higher truth reality. To take life in fully, you need to acknowledge that you were given the greatest gift any person can give you; this is the gift of life. This life we carry within us often comes to us from amazing stories throughout the ancestors' line. To walk through the storm of transition from the old story to the new story in gratitude and grace starts by taking your life in full. This can only come when we are able to say to our parents, "Thank you for giving me this life. I carry it fully in me, this flame that has been passed onto me and walked through the old story and never went out. I stand here with honour and respect knowing that I am from the family of light and I am here to ignite and expand this light so it can create a new world to live in." The separation of the light is what often stands strong between you and your parents. You are ambassadors to the light, opening to a higher truth, and you will see the innocence of yourself, your parents, and your ancestral line.

This is a very exciting time, and as you connect to the new grid, you will link back to me, your mother, and build a telepathic communication with me. It will be like having your own radio station where you can tune into and open to information and new ways of living. The natural flow and vibration of life from me, your mother, is often opposite to how you have and do life. The evolution process that you are in the process of experiencing is to live in the highest aspect of your true being. You do not need to worry about becoming this being, for you are already this. You just need to remember. The transition is a dimensional shift that will lessen the density of the reality you presently live in.

You are magnificent beings of the family of light, and you have come to me, Mother Earth, at this time as pioneers to assist with this most exciting time in your history. In order to make change and to assist in the journey of transition, and with it having a sense of gratitude, feeling blessed for your awakening and your own journey of transformation, honour all of this. Know your transformation and your knowledge was never here to make you bigger than anyone, it is here for the expansion of humanity. What you have done is opened the door and walked through, therefore going first.

I have to say that when my activation took place, gratitude and blessings were not my reality, and I said for a long time that if I had anything to do with this experience, I was drunk or pushed into agreeing to do it. The information and the knowing was just so out there for me that my journey has always been about surrender and acceptance. Even in writing this book, I have had to surrender to the process, and it would have been much easier for me not do it and to spend more time with my grandchildren and family.

The natural flow of life is often very opposite to how we do life, and often I felt I had no choice in what I was experiencing in my transformation. I felt like my will was taken over, and I remember saying that what I wanted felt like it had no importance. Yet what was being taught out in the community was that we could be what we wanted if we just have the intention, the dedication, the commitment, and we could create it. What I was experiencing was the opposite. I did not want the knowledge, the knowing, and I definitely did not want to go out and talk about this information. Writing a book was the most ridiculous thing I have ever considered. I never passed one English test at school, and I am dyslectic. I have had many tantrums and learnt to swear a lot to cope with the journey of acceptance and surrender and to have gratitude and know that I am blessed.

There is a natural flow taking place, and it feels like being on a boat on a river, floating downstream and going with the flow. Sometimes the flow is fast as it goes through rapids. Sometimes the flow nearly stops as it goes into places that have rocks and boulders in the river. Sometimes it is peaceful. Sometimes you flow to the riverbank, and you can get off for a while, and then the flow calls again, and you hop back in the boat. If you get confused and don't want to go at the speed or to the place where the flow takes you, sometimes you will try to go upstream. It can be difficult, as you are going in the opposite direction to the flow, letting go of how you want to be.

This journey is not about who you thought you were and what you think you are here to do. If someone had told me I was here with a message for humanity, that I would be an author and a speaker, I would have thought they were mad. The journey and the flow of my life were very opposite to what I wanted. My only choice was to let go and surrender to what was being birthed within me. It has taken me many years to stop the struggle and trust the flow. Trusting the flow of life is not about not taking action when you are in a rapid or when the river of life is flowing fast like it is now. It is about moving with the flow of the river. It may take you to places where your intellect will question why, and it may feel really uncomfortable at times. If you can stand in those times with gratitude in your heart, strength, and courage, you will know that the flow of life is about being in a place of acceptance, surrender, peace, and expansion.

In this time of transition from the old way to the new way, many may feel confused and question what direction is needed in their life. Some will experience what they thought they were here for is now not flowing for them. Know that you are here to be of service and assist humanity in this time; it is bigger than you. Surrender to the flow of life and take the mother's hand, and she will take you home. Separation of reality has lived in all of us, and it is a part of the divisions and a depletion of the old way, the old story. We live separated from the truth of our being inside of us, and this part of us that has been hidden and silenced is now starting to be heard. Your being is aligned to the mother, to each other, and is being birthed as a new story, a new way of living.

In the walk through the storm, we must accept that we will all go through the realms of our own destiny. The journey of the light is being honoured. As many have learnt that we create our own reality, this is often difficult to understand when we look at the starving children or the abused children and wonder, How could we create this reality? We are all a part of the whole, and there is no separation. We are all a part of the creation of what is experienced on Mother Earth. Honour the light, honour the life force and what amazing walks humanity has walked. Bow your head in reverence for the starving child. Honour this child, as every one of them shows us we are a race of people who have forgotten. Tell them they are a beacon of light and will shine out for humanity to see. If humanity cannot see the extraordinary light dynamics of the separation, more children will come offering themselves up to show us the way. Look into their eyes and say the game is over. Say we are all a part of the family of light, and what have we done to you, your own heart will cry out with the pain. A new vision is being born, and there is no more separation. I am you, you are me, and we are one.

As the old ways are breaking down, some systems just won't work. They won't provide the solution to global and community crises. Some of the old structures will open up and walk through the doorway of expansion, creating a bridge between the old ways and the new ways. Division is over, and a new way of connection and community will expand. In the transition, fear and confusion can escalate as the old story is leaving, especially for the masses that have no idea what is happening from the place of evolution. This crisis is a birth, not depletion, and new information needs to have credibility and acceptance to help the masses. That is why it is important for new leaders to stand up, providing education.

All things are a part of the whole, and humanity is innocent. I felt so sad when I opened to this information, for I could feel the innocence of all of us. I remember saying out loud one day, "How do people prepare for something they don't even know exists? How do you give this information to people? They will think you are mad!" It is like telling them the sky is not blue. I remember crying, thinking about the good people I know and the good people that are just like me. Ordinary people who have believed the reality they have been born into. How were these people going to live through this amazing time of change? I thought of the beautiful children and them being so trusting. I now realise that what we are living through does not have to be a nightmare if we can accept and surrender to a higher truth. The natural activation is in process, and this will create a great stirring for the masses. People will open up much more easily than they have ever done so before. The sleep we have all been in is over, and the awakening is in place.

There is a natural flow to this time of transition, and to enter this flow with ease and grace, we will need to see the innocence of humanity. We will need to understand how blessed we are to finally reach this time of completion, to understand how amazing our old story is and the ancestors' ability to hold onto the light through the struggle of life of the old story. Pioneers heard the call, opened the doorway, and now humanity is being asked to walk through. Do not be afraid, for what is leaving is not the truth of you. Sacredness, honour, and divinity are the flow of the new story.

There has been an intervention from the galactic world for this time of transition for humanity. We are being looked after, and we have all agreed to do this shift. Yes, there will be many that will have tantrums just like me, as many love the old ways, the old story. There is a natural flow coming back to us, and the transition and the walk through this storm can be a walk of grace and gratitude, for we are going home.

A New Story

Millions have been called and said yes.
Before you came into your body,
you committed to this new story for humanity.
Coding and blueprint would be activated
at this time in your evolution.
Then you came into your body and forgot.
Some have the knowing of the divine plan.
They are part of something
much bigger happening on
Mother Earth.

12

The New Story

Humanity—the time is now. The birth of 2012 was a springboard for us to rise from. Time stood strong in the old story, and it now calls out to us. Evolution is at hand here, and the time clock is running out. The old way is leaving, and the birth of the new story is in process. Time says, "I cannot hold this back. Get together, be ready, for it is now and urgent."

The pioneers are being asked to stand and lead humanity at this time. Many of you have been asked to be leaders to show humanity a new way. Yes, it is challenging and confronting because many of you are ordinary people that first heard this call of change. Align with your truth, trust the flow of life, and put action into place for the change. We need to move forward, as time is demanding change. The story is bigger; light is standing and holding up the pioneers who are assisting humanity to move forward.

The masses are innocent and have no reality or understanding of the time we are living in. The systems that have always provided solutions and stability have no information in them about this time in humanity's evolution. Many of the mass population will stir in this transition time, so it is important for the new leaders to stand up and show themselves, holding the light for a vision for the masses for a new way and a new world for the human race. This is all perfect and all on time. New ways are needed for the issues that need to be addressed globally, such as the environment, energy, human rights, disease, poverty, over population, money markets, etc. The new leaders that are men and women who align with a higher order of doing things and know that we are all connected and one race of people. People may live in different countries with different cultures and ways of living, yet we are all connected together under the family of humanity.

Thought thinks that our old beliefs stand strong, with a smile of control and a feeling of authority. Its vibration of operation is holding on tightly, not bending and not wanting to hear the call of change. Its communication is words of ridicule and stupidity about the new leaders of today. It looks down on the heart with pity and judgment. Thought states with all its power, "I have nothing to lose here. I am the position and reality of power on Mother Earth. I have been in authority for a long time, and nothing is going to change. All is happening in my time."

The evolutionary clock shakes it head and thinks, *How can this part of humanity not see the games of power that are played out? How foolish is thought to believe it can control time, Mother Earth, and the activation? It has no idea what is happening at this time.*

The doorway is open for the human race to walk through. An electromagnetic energy force field has been activated, and Mother Earth is pulling us back home. She is calling to her children, telling them that they have arrived at a new cycle of human existence. This is a time of change, transition, a letting go of the old ways, and a birthing of the new ways.

Separation is leaving, and it has served us well. It has helped create the world we live in today and has been a part of our evolution. It gave us a place of order and control and space to see the bigger picture. Without it, we would not have reached this amazing time of completion and expansion, seeing light and dark, good and bad, sad and happy, God and evil, and all things in separation. This has bought us to this time of expansion. The game of separation was put in place eons ago, and in the activation, our DNA codes of remembrance will activate, and we will remember our blueprint. Separation is not the truth of us. It has lived with us as an illusion that we have believed, and it is time for it to go. You are me, I am you, and we are one. This is the new story.

The pole shift that many have talked about in our time of evolution is the pole shift to the heart operating in its power, connecting to all things, linking back to the mother, connecting to each other, connecting to galactic worlds and the divinity of self. Thought will be asked to let go and bow its head and serve the power connection of the heart. In the transition, the heart will have many stories to tell about the domination, devaluation, and manipulation it has felt and the numbness for its survival. There are many pioneers of this time that have told their heart stories and healed the pain inside. They have created businesses that provide sacred spaces for people to express their stories with respect and honour the old stories and the old way. The old pain cannot come through to the new story. The heart often could not feel the light, as it was covered up, and it lived many days in the old ways of persecution, denial, and having no access to its own love and beauty.

The activation says, "What you say and what you do will not stop what is happening on Mother Earth." Your DNA codes of remembrance do not come from your thought process. Your thoughts and your present human reality have no decision in this natural process, for it is bigger. The activation is part of your evolutionary process, on time, and in perfect alignment with the new grid. This information is a knowing and is coming into form as communication is aligned with a higher truth. There are no facts or proof, and to many, this knowledge may sound ridiculous. That is fine. Yet there are many people that are feeling the alignment who don't need proof.

The grid supplies a free and unending amount of energy to those who connect to it. Aligning with this higher energy and connecting to Mother Earth, you will find that this energy is a frequency and a web system of light connecting to the new grid system of an electromagnetic force field. You will feel the vibration in your nervous system as a rearrangement takes place in your physical body. Sometimes you may wake up at night and literally feel the rearrangement taking place. You are aligning with the new grid, a web system of light that operates from thought waves that serve the heart space. Many may find their physical body needing help, as the density of the old vibration is often very difficult to let go of. As the new frequency expands in the physical body, our physical, emotional, and mental bodies that have all operated from the frequency of the old energy, from the energy of the old story and the old way, will need to have some understanding to allow this new frequency to expand in a place of gratitude and grace. What we are experiencing is amazing. It is enormous compared to the reality of operation in the old story. It is scientific, yet beyond the science of today. If you find your body is in a place of being challenged, overwhelmed, and in overload, there are health practitioners available to help align the energy systems within the human body. These health practitioners can be found in holistic complementary well-being websites or local health magazines or newspapers in communities.

Mother Earth is holding the place of wisdom, innocence, and humility for this time at hand. She is calling us all. She has her hand on the pioneers, asking them to show humanity how to move forward. She has her connection to the heart, and she says to it, "Stand up and feel your truth and connection." She has eyes on humanity, knowing all is in place and in its right order. She sees the birth taking place and the children feeling safe and aligned with a new world of this time. She, our Mother Earth, understands the bigger picture, and she is holding out her hand for humanity to take it.

Time is calling out loudly and now saying to the masses, "Change is here. Stand up and walk through the doorway. The old story needs to go. Those pioneers that are holding the light and the lost knowledge—it is not to make them more important, it's not to make them bigger and better, it is for the service of humanity. To separate ourselves from each other is the old game and the memory of the separation. Know that the separation is leaving now, for it was on a timeframe of evolution, and the illusion cannot be a part of the new birth."

The ancestors are all observing the interactions taking place. What a journey they have had to bring this time in place for the human race.

Their connection to their family lines is strong, on purpose, and they celebrate the reconnection of the human global family.

Thought is feeling weaker, a little out of control, and it will hang on to the authority of control for as long as it can. Many more people are stirring and hearing the call. The numbers are growing in this transitional time, and many are feeling something big is happening, and many don't understand. The winds of change are showing themselves, and many of the old structures are wobbly and are in the process of aligning with the new frequency being birthed. It is becoming difficult to hold on to the old way, as we are all a part of the energy systems of Mother Earth, and these systems are expanding naturally, extending outwards further and further as the electromagnetic force field is interconnection and expanding.

The heart is getting stronger, and the light is standing next to the heart. The heart is remembering it came first, before the thought. When we look at the scan of a new born baby, we see and hear the heartbeat, for it comes first into creation, as it is a part of the pulsation of creation and operates and lives in connection.

Humanity is innocent. This is a vibration of truth. Some are frightened, as a natural stirring is happening for many and they ask what is happening.

A birth is taking place that is a natural process of evolution. Time is a part of an evolving process, and we are all witness to this most amazing time in human history where our DNA is activating, and we are starting to remember the bigger picture of our existence. The people of love and light are holding the flame of truth once again. The power source, the heart, is taking back its position of connection, and thought is standing next to the heart with total respect and honour for the vibration of connection. Thought's amazing ability to manifest its reality has a purpose of service for humanity. What an amazing time to be born in, as we have the ability to create a new world to live in. Many opportunities will open for humanity to create new ways of living life through connection.

145

We are living in transition with one foot in the old story and the other in the new story. Some cannot let go of the old way, and this in fine and acceptable. In time, all will be revealed to us, as this transitional time is a journey that humanity will need to take, such as letting go of what was, walking over the bridge, and entering the new story. The birth is anchored, and a new vibration of human reality is now in place here on Mother Earth. Many have been a part of the birthing process, which was a natural pulsation of evolution beating the rhythm of this new story. A higher truth will be felt by many, and their natural instincts will align with this higher truth that is beating inside of them. The electromagnetic force field is in a place of expansion. Understanding this natural process from a scientific point of view, new pioneers of the science of today will bring facts about this natural state of expansion being experienced by humanity.

The pain of the past will be heard as the heart speaks its truth. New ways will birth from this, and the heart will stands in its power in each of us. As we start to understand that something big is happening on Mother Earth, giving this natural process credibility, a global acceptance will come.

The New Woman

Women hold a flame of light, and it was passed down to them from women before them. Many women of today are in the process of healing the lies and illusions in their heart. The birth of an energy of connection will change the operation and daily life of women globally.

To unplug the old story in us and for us to be a part of the creation of a new story, the vibration of love is the answer. This vibration is expanding in us as we let go and heal the stories and pain of the past. As we are able to view and understand the bigger picture of our family lines, we will acknowledge that love became severed from life's traumas. Feelings of forgiveness, peace, acceptance, love, and gratitude are ways of moving forward. Know that our family heritage operated in a place of separation and disconnection and that the human race has been operating from this place.

The new woman knows that the feminine is freeing herself for the greater good of humanity. Nurturing, intuition, sacredness, connection, collaboration, wisdom, respect, honour, courage, commitment, and love all have a high place of order and position of authority to open up pathways to expand life on Mother Earth. The new woman will support all women on Mother Earth, and her sisters will be seen in all countries and places not separated from herself. She will stand next to women who have no voice and say, "I am your voice." The new woman will stand next to the women who are devalued and say, "The feminine has a higher purpose, and it is for her to expand in all of humanity." She will resonate with the heartbeat of Mother Earth, knowing that all the children on Mother Earth are a part of the family of humanity. This will grow stronger with the new woman as she aligns to the new grid and opens herself to a higher truth. Her heart will take backs its power, and it will stand strong with courage and commitment, for the energy vibration of the grid is love and the sacredness of life. She will stand in a court of law, she will stand in the political arena, and she will say, "A new story for humanity has arrived. It is in my heartbeat and connects me to all things. The old games are over, and finally we can start to live a new way of life. No more starving children, no more devaluation of human life, and human rights will have the highest place of service, for we are all connected."

Many new leaders will be women in this time of transition, for women held the position of the heart in the game of separation, and it is the heartbeat that is the entrance to the new story. Community will be very important, and the women will come forth feeling supported by each other. The women's ancestral lines that have walked this journey generation after generation stand strong behind the women of today. There are tears and gratitude here for all women, and the knowing is we have finally reached a time where women of the world now have a voice. They now have true power, for it comes from a place of connection. Women are remembering who they are, and the commitment to unplugging the old story has been extraordinary. The desire for the heart to be free has been a driving force in this freedom. Love will have its place of position and power, and humanity will understand it is love that is the force of the electromagnetic field that is in all of us. It is like the glue that keeps us all together.

The New Man

He has walked a long journey home and has always been companied by the old reality. He has had to go very deep to find his truth, for he was taken away from it eons ago. Great courage has been needed for the man who has heard the call to release the order of authority from the heart. To have the strength to go to this place in the man's journey of evolution is honoured by the new woman. She sees his innocence, and she understands that his rights to own his heartbeat were denied to him. The old man was birthed from this place of denial and separated from the connection to love. He was used and abused to create a world of domination. There is a lot of rage and anger in the man needing to be healed, as it cannot come to birth the new story for the new man.

The new man operates from a truth deep inside him, having very little connection to the old reality. Sometimes this has created difficulties in his life and a feeling of isolation from the man society of the old story. He has felt the pain of the devaluation of the feminine on Mother Earth, for this is a part of him too. Feelings of not belonging to the man culture and feelings of not fitting in have often have been a part of the journey, as the new man does not want to do it like the men before him.

The birth for the new man comes from a place of understanding and honouring the fathers before him, knowing the courage and strength the men had to reach in this time in evolution. The man lines in our families and ancestors feel great honour to stand behind their sons. They feel the tears, and they feel the heartbeat of the new man with great pride and respect, giving their blessing for the new story to birth the new man and to open to new ways of living. The new man is linking back to our Mother Earth, aligning with the new grid, and opening to a higher truth all for the purpose of harmony and wholeness for humanity. The new man stands next to his partner with love and respect, and he is here to create a world where the children know they are safe and loved. In the natural alignment taking place, the new man will feel the heartbeat of life and demand new ways in our social, economic, and political arenas. Many will feel pulled to the interconnection of all things, and they will create new ways of living.

In the transitional time that we are living in now, we need strong leaders to walk the journey with humanity to create the new story. The new man knows and trusts the natural flow of life, and he is not here to make the old way wrong. He has great respect here and bows his head in reverence for what has been before him. He is here to open up a new way of living, knowing that the games of power have been made up from the appetite of a few and the mass population has often been in states of powerlessness. The new man knows and accepts the birth of a higher truth that has taken place, and he is here to protect this birth. He knows he is a part of this natural process taking place, but he knows that he is not the ruler of it. He is the protector holding a sacred space for the growth and expansion to take place. He stands strong, his heart is clear, and he speaks from the vibration of his truth, which is love. This love is courage, compassion, humility, and integrity, and it operates from a whole new paradigm of existence. He states with full power that he is here to serve and bring about new ways in all our systems, to bring about solutions for the issues that humanity faces in their families, communities, and countries. We are all interconnected, and he knows this with full commitment. The pulsation of evolution runs through his veins, and his higher purpose has been heard. He is in flight mode like an eagle soaring high and bringing about change for higher good for humanity.

The New Child

For the new child, when you are put into your mother's arms, the new woman and the new man will say to you, "How blessed we are to have you come into our lives. We will learn much from you. Your connection, your wisdom, and truth belong to you. You know who you are now." The new man will say, "I will love and protect you so you are free to explore your own truth." The new woman will say, "You are love, and you carry the light. I am here for you to expand the love and light and watch you grow to be all you can be."

There is a new story birthing on Mother Earth, and the children will feel safe and protected. This is the new way.

Education will change. Know that when a child is connected to their truth and is standing in love, they have the ability to expand and create. As individuals, we will not deplete a child and tell them who they are not. This game is over, and it belongs to the old story.

In the new story, a child will not be expected to carry the pain from their parents, for the new adults will take responsibility for what they create. This is the new way of living. Information about being responsible for one's life is being taught by pioneer teachers now, taking life in full from the parent, as the life force is received generation after generation, honouring the ancestors. Our world will start to see a bigger picture operate from a new paradigm and new ways of living. In time, the masses will understand that the game of separation and the games of power operated in the old story.

Many of the children being born now have the knowing and the connection upon arriving on Mother Earth. They will be a part of creating a new world for humanity and are vision holders for the light.

The children on Mother Earth from all countries and cultures have rights, and these rights will be heard. This is the new story, and when the old control of our thought lets go, and our thoughts begin to serve the power of our heart, the staving and abuse of children on Mother Earth will end. The responsibility for the children of this earth belongs to all of us.

The New Family

The new family operates from the place of connection, knowing it is a part of humanity's family, and they will respect and honour the generations before them. Family connects to the cycle of life, and the cycle of the family is never destroyed. Some leave for a while, and some new people come into the family, yet the cycle of life remains always. No one is excluded from the cycle, as universal laws are in place. Love is the energy of exchange, and the children are always protected. The parents come first, and they give life, and children take life in full from them.

New ways for families to live include an understanding of responsibility for the self. Self-determinism is taken back in the new family life. A right to live one's life fully is a birth right, and learning new ways for families to expand their reality about relationships, health, wealth, and well-being is a part of the new family.

In the activation, so much will change, and all the old stories need to be let go of, birthing the new way when the heart is connected. Thought serving this connection will totally change our daily existence. Community will be a big part of the new family.

Some may feel like our very structures of moral and goodness is going as the shift and change is being experienced in our daily lives and in our relationships. Same-sex relationships are being expressed openly, marriage and family breakdown is accelerating, and cultural beliefs are being challenged. Our whole reality of family is being shaken up, which is giving us new opportunities to expand our reality of family and love. New ways of living life will evolve through the DNA codes being activated and a birth of the vibration of love.

The New Business

The old ways are leaving, and no position of the old authority can interfere or stop this natural process. Something bigger is happening on Mother Earth. It is scientific, yet there is no scientific fact in our present reality. Many will try to hang on to the old ways, having no information about the birth taking place. This birth is an electromagnetic force activation, and it is something that cannot be controlled or manipulated.

New ways of business are in the process of birth. There will be an understanding of the connection to each other, a linking back to our Mother Earth and the divinity of self. It is a vibration and a new energy of operation that is calling.

Walking forward to the new story will provide new ways of exchange, and ethics and the highest good will be put in place. Many old ways of doing business will not come through to the new story, for it is a new vibrational frequency, and the old ways cannot live in this new frequency. Pioneers that have heard the call are putting new ways into business in our world today. There will be education to the masses about money, and the old beliefs about the lack and the greed of money will be asked to leave. Many of us carry from our ancestry line the beliefs and reality about money. In the new story, money will be understood as an energy exchange and that it can be a force of beauty, love, and expansion. In the old story, it was used to control and manipulate the masses, and this game will stop in the new story.

Our responsibility to the global family will show itself in the new story, and we will remember that this natural process of evolution is bigger than the business that is a bureaucratic system of the old story. This is all on a timeframe of evolution.

The Masses of Humanity

Many do not hear the call and are locked into the old vibration. The old story is their truth of existence. Many will leave this life locked into this old reality in their natural time of death, as they were not able to understand or hear the call, for the old story is too strong in them.

The masses of humanity will see change all around them, yet the old ways are where they feel they belong. In this time, a birth is taking place, and in the time of transition, some will not come through to the new ways, as they do not choose to activate their DNA codes of remembrance. They are innocent, and the cycle of life will provide a natural process for them to leave. In the new story, the human reality of life and death will be expanded, and in our understanding of this natural process, we will know that death is not what we have been told. It is a new beginning and a continuation of your individual evolution.

For millions of others, they did agree to hear the call, and there will be a mass stirring globally. Confusion and fear could be a daily reality in this time of transition if you do not understand what is happening. There has been great preparation for this time of birth of a new story. This preparation has been at hand in the last few decades, and what you have known as your truth and reality is now at an end of time. There is information and education available if a deeper understanding is needed. A doorway has been opened for you to walk through. Wow, what extraordinary times to be living in!

Vision for a New World

Awakening, knowing, and healing are coming forth.
Humanity is blessed as
Your heart has called you
To remember
Freedom.
Development of a higher mind is on time.
Global family is who we are.

The place of power is in the heartbeat, and it is a part of the electromagnet force field that is a part of all things. This is the place of interconnection, and this is power that has not had its place of recognition and respect in our earthly history. We do not know or understand it, for there is no evidence within the intellectual structures about this amazing power force.

Our human heart has had a journey throughout all of our history in a place of powerlessness. There is a lot of pain in the human heart, and as it speaks this pain, it communicates to us daily, telling us over and over again who we are. It speaks words of devaluation and manipulation. It expresses what culture and society tell us about the pain that devalues and judgers others. It communicates with us, telling us who we are, and then we share this pain with others. The human heart is crying and is dying, as we have no value for human life. It has reached a place in our human evolution that it is calling to the masses to free it.

The call is coming from a pulsating force field that beats to the same rhythm as Mother Earth's heartbeat. The electromagnetic grid lines have been activated, and she, our Mother Earth, has heard the call of evolution. In the bigger picture, it is enormous, yet we have no information or ability to comprehend the enormity of the bigger picture of human evolution. In order to have an understanding of a bigger picture, we use our thinking and intellect and put it into different boxes, dissect it, and experiment with it, believing we have it under control and are in charge of it. The evolutionary pulse has been pulling a small percentage of the human population to feel the electromagnetic force field in a place of activation. Pioneers of our day have been working extremely hard over the last few decades opening the human heart.

Humanity has a heritage, and it has forgotten that it is our birth right to have this heritage back. We are much more than we understand, and our DNA has a place of remembrance from long ago that we will remember in the activation taking place. The activation is on a timeframe of evolution, and expansion is its call. The electromagnetic force field is in a place of alignment, taking us back home to our truth. All of this is scientific, yet it is beyond the science of today. In time, future pioneer scientists will bring this information to the masses to give an understanding as to what is taking place. The activation can have physical, mental, and emotional implications for the human who is experiencing it, for this is a physical, mental, and emotional expansion.

The stirring for the masses is at hand now, for it is time. Birth of the new vibration is here and now. A doorway has been opened by the pioneers for humanity to walk through. The whole human race has been locked behind this doorway in all of our history, living like prisoners of a reality, living like the only existence in the universe, living with God outside of ourselves, and having no connection to self, each other, or Mother Earth.

The evolutionary electromagnetic pulsation is a part of all there. It is a higher order of truth and reality, and it has nothing to do with a thought or our human intellect. Our thinking does not know or understand what is happening, and the human reality thinks it has it all in control. What is happening is much bigger than the thought of humans. The power structures in place on Mother Earth cannot stop or interfere with this natural evolutionally process taking place. It is all on a timeframe of evolution.

The opening of the human heart is the entrance to the new story. As we unplug from the old story, the pain, deception, and lies in our heart will be free, and we will get stronger and stand in our truth.

First there is vibration, and everything is this. Next comes image, and then comes words of our native tongue as we remember this is how we express and communicate. The natural evolutional pulse that is within humanity's heartbeat is a part of the electromagnetic force field that is a part of all that is. On a time mechanism of evolution, the electromagnetic grid lines are in a place of activation that is a natural process of humanity's evolution. We knew this before we were born. We knew this was a time of extraordinary change for humanity, and we were capable of evolving to understand a bigger picture of who we are. Everything is energy, and within our DNA, activation codes of memory rise up within us. The heart cannot hold the old story in it, for the energy in the heart is expanding through the electromagnetic force field, and it can't hold onto anything that does not align with the new vibration that is birthing in humanity. The pulsation of the heartbeat is in and out, and is directly aligned with Mother Earth. There is no separation, and this pull is pulling us back to her naturally. It is a part of the flame of life, a force field bringing to it all that it needs for its next stage of expansion. This force field is electromagnetic like a magnet, aligning everything in its path. We are moving to a higher order of truth, for the vibration can see what the vibration is. It is like we have been asleep, able to understand and see only what was available to us as a race of people that vibrated at a vibration below two hundred. A natural evolutionary process is taking place and an activation of memory.

As the pulsation in the heart is felt through the electromagnetic force field, all will align to expand it, and this is the next stage in our human evolution.

The pulsating pull will take you to people, places, and things that expand your reality. It is a natural flow of life, yet we often still feel comfortable living out of step, making up our own flow of existence. We are at a crossroads with global issues presenting themselves, from climate change to human rights. The present reality of life does not have the answers, and often our intellect will be in a state of panic, for it has made up all the avenues of survival for humanity. In this crossroad that we are living in now, we will question and often ask if we will survive. We will find solutions to our present issues through an expansion of consciousness.

The electromagnetic force field is magnetic, bringing into itself all it needs, pulling in magnetically for its expansion of evolution. The picture is bigger than we think. The access to the higher order of truth is the human heart that has been misused and abused. It is the power place, for it is the place of interconnection and the place of the electromagnet force field.

When we have our heritage back as a human race, we will remember our connection to love and light. When our heart is free, it will translate this vibration of love to us in a higher order of life, for the true essence of this love is the sacredness of life, all pulsating and pulling us home in a natural flow of life. The magnetic force field is pulling to us what is needed for this transition taking place.

We are aligning with a new grid of energy, and it operates from a universal law opening to a higher truth. Our DNA codes are in activation, and we will remember that we are holding the light. It will ignite and expand this vibration of love, and we will create unity, connection, cooperation, collaboration, and community in a new way.

A great turning point is here, and we are living in this amazing time where there is a shift from the industrial growth society to a life-sustaining civilisation. Ecologists, activists, visionaries, scientists, indigenous leaders, many ordinary men and women, and pioneers of our day all have heard the call. The winds of change are gathering for the purpose of creating a new story for humanity, for our children, for the people of this world, and for the future generations to come.

When we are true to ourselves, future generations are blessed.

A vision, a new story, a global family. I am you, you are me, and we are one.

Glossary

Activation

Activation is within the electromagnetic force field of evolution, and it has nothing to do with our thoughts. The activation is triggering our DNA codes, which will allow us to have a natural memory surface of who we are and align us to a higher truth.

Electromagnetic Force Field

This is a powerful force and a part of all creation. It is the Earth's evolutionary path. The universal parade of stars is guided by a force higher than we can imagine. The picture is bigger, as we are more than a thought; we are a part of the electromagnetic force field.

Grid

This is an electromagnetic fulfilment of a higher plan and humanity's destiny, linking the world with the concept of oneness. This grid is a vibration, and it is an instrument of peace and love and will be used to build this world in the coming millenniums. Evidence of this grid is not in the old story. The grid is linked to the heart centre of an individual's web of light systems and is beyond the science of the old story. The electromagnetic grid within Mother Earth is at place of activation, and this was implemented from the pulsation of evolution. She, our mother, is pulling us home to remember who she is and who we are.

Heart

The heart is a symbol of love globally. The human heartbeat is the natural place of pulsation. The heart is the entry to the next stage in human evolution, for it is a part of the electromagnetic force field that is a part of all that is. The evolutionary pulse is felt here within the heart. The heart is the power source, and we have never understood this in the old story of humanity.

Heritage

Humanity has a heritage that we have forgotten, and within the pulsation of evolution and the activation of memory, we will take back a power and truth that we have forgotten. Our blueprint is from the people of love and light, and we separated from this aspect of ourselves and forgot who we are. We have the ability to take back our truth and understand a bigger picture of human existence.

New Story

A new way of looking at and experiencing life. A new beginning, expanding our reality of who we are, where we come from, and how we create life. A birth in process and part of humanity's evolution.

Old Story

History tells the story, the way that we have lived and understood human existence through all centuries. We are living in a time of completion of this old story. It is an ending and finishing of how it has been.

Pioneers

There is a small percentage of the population that can hear the winds of change and feel the pulsation of evolution in their heartbeat. Through an activation of a deep memory of who they are, courage and commitment has been asked of them. Many have new information and new ways of living birthing inside of them. They have information that is often in opposition to the old story of human existence, for the old story came from a place of separation and disconnection. The only qualification that is needed for the pioneer is to hear their heartbeat, for the new story is birthed from a pulsation of evolution and is not a decision or choice of thought from human reality.

Separation

We have lived from a place of separation and disconnection in all the history of human reality. We are separate from God, each other, Mother Earth, and the universal worlds. We have created a world to live in from this place of separation, and the pulsation of evolution is pulling us to expand and see the truth that we are not separate and that we are interconnected to all people, places, and things.

Thought

The thought has created the present world we live in, and our intellect has made up all the rules. The thought process has all the power, and it has always stood above the heart place. It has evolved and informed us of great new science and education, providing us with the lifestyles we live today.

Timeframe of Evolution

We live with two timeframes:

1. The Gregorian calendar, which is twenty-four hours in a day and twelve months in a year
2. A pulsation of evolution where we are living at the birth of a new story

Transition

This is existing with one foot in the old story and one foot in the new story. It is on a timeframe of evolution, not the time that humanity has made up.

About the Author

Susan Altschwager is an evolutionary teacher, writer, Family Constellations facilitator, trained rebirther, and public speaker. She self-published her first book, *An Ordinary Woman's Extraordinary Journey,* in 2001 and has spoken at several state and international rebirthing conferences. Susan currently resides with her family in South Australia.